SHOWING YOUR COLORS

SHOWING YOUR colors

A Designer's Guide to Coordinating Your Wardrobe

Jeanne Allen

Chronicle Books • San Francisco

First published in the United States 1986
by Chronicle Books

Copyright © 1985 by Kawade Shobo
Shinsha Publishers. All rights reserved.
No part of this book may be reproduced
in any form without written permission
from the publishers.

Printed in Japan.

Color Coordination by Ikuyoshi
Shibukawa and Yumi Takahashi was
first published in Japan by Kawade
Shobo Shinsha Publishers.

Library of Congress
Cataloging in Publication Data

Allen Jeanne, 1945–
Showing your colors.
1. Color in clothing.   I. Title.
TT507.A64   1986   646'.34   86-2656
ISBN 0-87701-381-0

Edited by Terry Ryan

Distributed in Canada by
Raincoast Books
112 East 3rd Avenue
Vancouver, B.C.
V5T 1C8

10   9   8   7   6   5   4   3   2

Chronicle Books
San Francisco, CA

TABLE OF CONTENTS

Introduction

The American way of dress is based on coordinated sportswear. In the seventies, fashion designers dictated which skirt went with which jacket; in the eighties, American women have become their own designers and coordinators. Gone are the days of fashion directives from Seventh Avenue. Now designers who wish to be around next season must offer new ideas as well as new options—in length, style, texture, and color. From these new fashions, American women will take note of the "news," buy an eyedropper's worth of what is offered, and most likely combine what is new with the clothes they already own.

At Jeanne-Marc, a new collection begins when we select the color palette for the upcoming season. From this initial step, it will be nearly one year before these same colors hit the runway in New York as a coordinated collection of sportswear. In many respects, choosing the season's new colors is the most critical moment in the development of the collection. These eight or ten colors will be contrasted and combined into prints and wovens that will become the textiles from which the fabrics will take shape: first on paper as sketches, then in the round and real as jackets, skirts, and dresses. In the end, the collection might be two hundred separate pieces. But one personality will prevail, and it will be the personality that was determined by those initial color choices.

Every fashion season has its favorite colors. As designers, we are often asked why one color becomes popular and how designers know which one it will be. What seems a great mystery is really a simple process of training the eye to look for and identify the colors that look exciting and fresh. We know that our first reaction to color is emotional, and we simply trust that reaction and follow what our eyes are telling us.

We at Jeanne-Marc are very excited by this book on color coordination. After using the other two books in the series, *Designer's Guide to Color* and *Designer's Guide to Color 2,* we are at last being offered a comprehensive presentation of color relationships that directly apply to fashion. Whether you are a professional in the field of fashion or a non-professional simply trying to get your wardrobe to make sense, the first step is choosing a basic color range to work within. Since very few people wear only one color, coordination becomes an immediate concern.

This compact book allows you to quickly scan more color possibilities than anyone could dream up in a year. You can also look at one color and see what happens when that color is paired with a series of different colors. What soon becomes obvious is that red has many more than one personality when paired first with black, then green, then white, and finally purple. This versatility suggests multiple ways in which a shirt or jacket from a past season can be made to look new when coordinated with a color not considered before. That perfectly wearable but boring blue skirt you have been pairing with a wine sweater can initiate a whole new look when combined with a yellow shirt and magenta accessories.

For the professional, this book is a great tool to quickly consider a wide range of color combinations that can become tomorrow's ready-to-wear. Unexpected mixing of color will leap off the page and beg to be given further consideration. For the non-professional, the book can be used to analyze, coordinate, and re-create an existing wardrobe with a look that is both personal and new.

How To Use This Book

Finding colors that work together in your wardrobe is a process that begins by selecting a basic color to work from, whether it be for a skirt, jacket, sweater, or pants. This basic color will be your starting point, and all additional colors will relate to this initial choice. Beginning with black, this book presents 53 colors, grouped according to tone and brightness. To see how any one of these particular colors relates to a variety of other colors, turn to the page number listed under each color. As you survey the 1380 color combinations now open to you, notice the ones that immediately draw your eye. Some of these combinations may be new to you, but if they are appealing, give them further consideration.

As you become familiar with this book, you will be able to scan the color combinations quickly and select those you like; this editing process will become almost automatic as you learn to trust your eye. Two things to remember: One, become sensitive to combinations you absolutely don't like — ask yourself why, and eventually you will begin to understand your own sense of color; two, know that your eye for color will develop a certain sophistication and be drawn to combinations you once dismissed as unappealing. After a time, we all grow tired of colors that become too popular — the eye seeks out the new and stimulating. That's what fashion is all about.

Color coordination is, of course, only one-third of the wardrobe development process. The other two considerations are shape and texture (or material). These last two subjects, however important, should only be considered after color selection is made.

In the basic color combinations shown in pages 4 through 95, blocks of color are presented with skirts, blouses, sweaters, and pants. Because you won't always be wearing solids, think about how these colors would look in print or plaid — which might be difficult at first. However, if you can envision how yellow flowers might look on a royal blue background, you will begin to use this book in a multidimensional way. Remember that your basic color is just that; any other color is an accent to that basic color. Sometimes you will be wearing two colors in equal amounts, as shown in the book. Many times, though, the right way to combine the colors will be in unequal ratios. Sometimes a black or white accent is suggested either in the illustration or the text. Notice how the dual combination changes character when a third color is added.

To further investigate these more complex — and realistic — combinations, look at the style and color coordinations that begin on page 96. Study the multiple variations to understand the diversity of choices open to you. You can use this book as a reference, but its real value will be in analyzing the illustrations and broadening your own color sense. From this process, you will be able to look at your own wardrobe with a fresh, creative eye.

The 53 basic colors illustrated and described in this book, their names and page numbers:

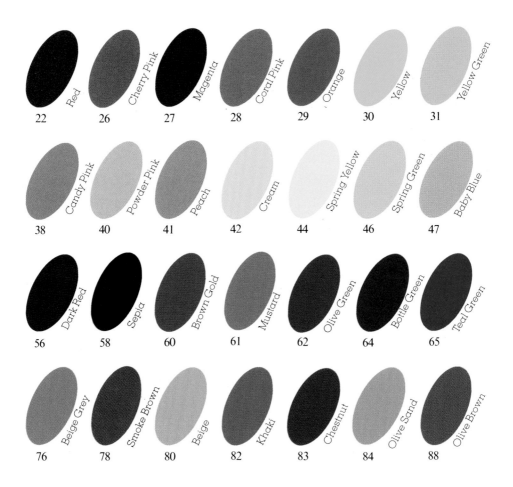

Red 22
Cherry Pink 26
Magenta 27
Coral Pink 28
Orange 29
Yellow 30
Yellow Green 31

Candy Pink 38
Powder Pink 40
Peach 41
Cream 42
Spring Yellow 44
Spring Green 46
Baby Blue 47

Dark Red 56
Sepia 58
Brown Gold 60
Mustard 61
Olive Green 62
Bottle Green 64
Teal Green 65

Beige Grey 76
Smoke Brown 78
Beige 80
Khaki 82
Chestnut 83
Olive Sand 84
Olive Brown 88

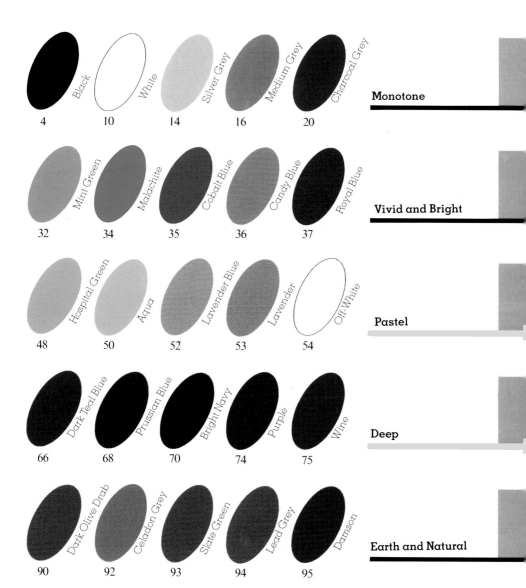

Black	White	Silver Grey	Medium Grey	Charcoal Grey
4	10	14	16	20

Monotone

Mint Green	Malachite	Cobalt Blue	Candy Blue	Royal Blue
32	34	35	36	37

Vivid and Bright

Hospital Green	Aqua	Lavender Blue	Lavender	Off-White
48	50	52	53	54

Pastel

Dark Teal Blue	Prussian Blue	Bright Navy	Purple	Wine
66	68	70	74	75

Deep

Dark Olive Drab	Celadon Grey	Slate Green	Lead Grey	Damson
90	92	93	94	95

Earth and Natural

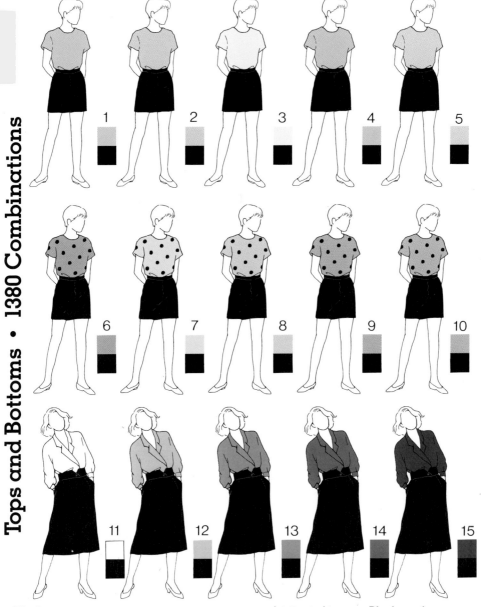

Black

Every season sees a new set of fashion colors come and go, but black consistently remains the most wearable color. For many years and in many cultures, black has been associated with death, old age, and somber events. Recently, however, particularly in Western culture, black has acquired a modern and sophisticated image. Black can be worn on its own to create a dramatic effect, but it is most often combined with other colors to make a special kind of fashion statement. Rather than acting as a neutral, black is a catalyst used with other colors to evoke a strong emotional response. Consider this color carefully and experiment with it to achieve

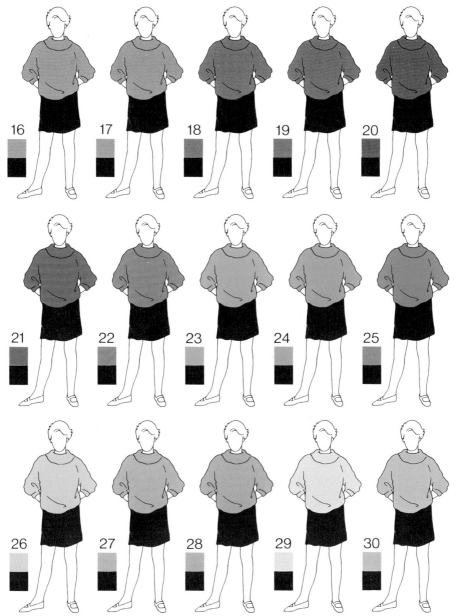

your individual look.

When black is combined with pastels (figures 1-10), the contrast creates a contemporary and sharp image. The first popular use of these combinations emerged in the fifties when black worn with pink—and to a lesser extent, with the other pastels—stood for youth and the new age. In the late seventies, black

and pastels came together again in punk and new wave fashion. To avoid the sharp, aggressive quality in this color combination, add white, and the prevailing image will be new and fresh.

In figures 11-15, you can see that monotone shades from white to charcoal grey combine easily with black. While the effect is on the somber side, it can

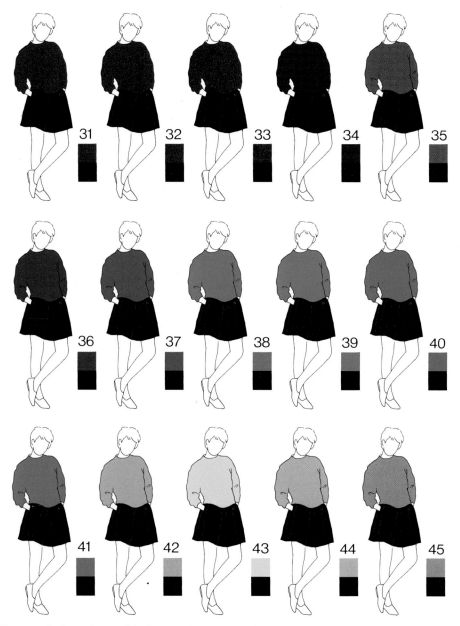

still be very fashion-forward (advanced), depending on the shapes and materials involved. The most graphic example of the effect of these combinations was the highly popular Japanese fashion that swept the West in 1982. The Japanese designers, for the most part, limited their color palette to black, grey, and white—but there was nothing conservative about their look.

In figures 16-30, black is used with middle tones of coral pink and heliotrope, creating somewhat the same problems as when black is used with pastels. You can keep away from a hard look by adding grey to the color combination. Grey softens and nicely unites any of these colors with black.

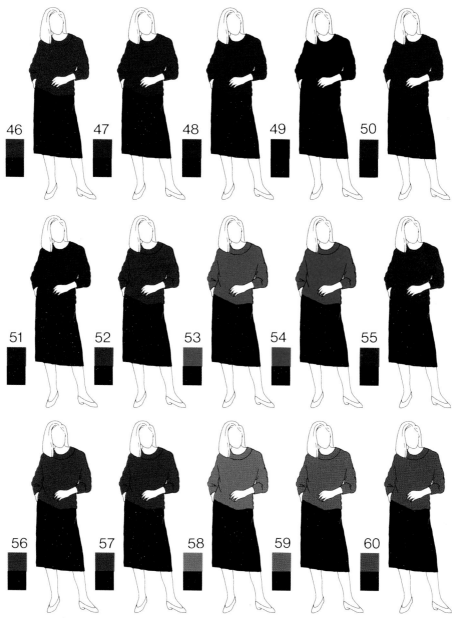

Undoubtedly the most popular way to wear black is to combine it with clear, bright colors (figures 31-45). The effect is dramatic and upbeat. The color is the thing; reds are redder and blues are brighter, overshadowing both the fabric and the shape of the garment. For spring and summer, the addition of white is often a nice freshener and makes the bright colors appear even more brilliant.

For fall and winter, black is frequently combined with darker colors such as the teal and mahogany mixes in figures 46-60. The effect is one of serious refinement. This kind of color palette is especially popular among business women who wish to wear some color

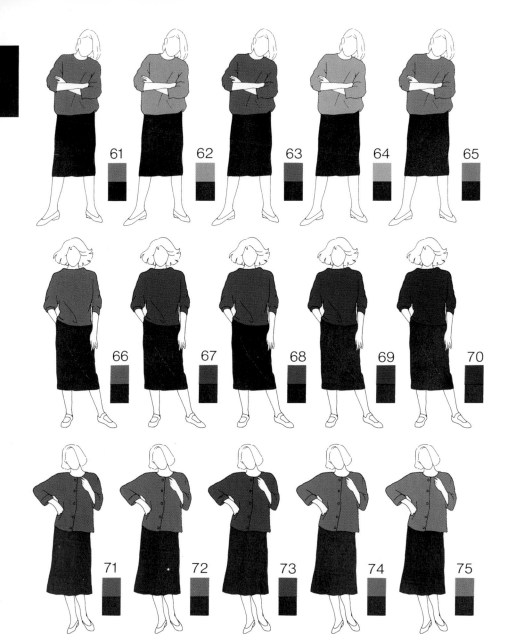

61 62 63 64 65

66 67 68 69 70

71 72 73 74 75

and still blend in with the prevailing muted atmosphere of a business-suit world. Carefully selected jewelry and accessories can contribute to a beautifully sophisticated look.

In figures 61-90, black is combined with muted tones. These combinations tend to appear drab and represent the least popular use of black and color in

women's wear. These colors are often seen in men's fashion and in men's-wear looks in women's fashion, but they are usually regarded as being either too sophisticated or too sober and matronly. Very striking looks can be achieved by coupling moss green and black, but here the material, shape, and accessories must be just right to avoid a

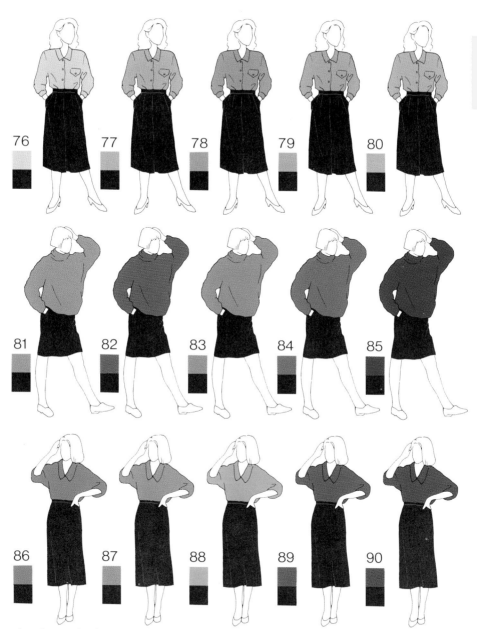

dowdy, washed-out look. A sure hand
and a good understanding of yourself
are needed to succeed here.

White

White is the only color that challenges black in popularity. Like black, white is actually a "non-color," an absence of color. In our minds, however, it is very much a color and an absolutely essential component of our wardrobes. White has multiple personalities and can evoke a certain look, depending on the colors it

is combined with. It is the perfect neutral, mixing easily with all colors *and itself*—consider white on white.

While white is often presented as a fashion color for winter, its real importance begins in the early spring when it can be combined with soft pastels. Mixed with pale yellow or pale pink, white heightens the lightness and

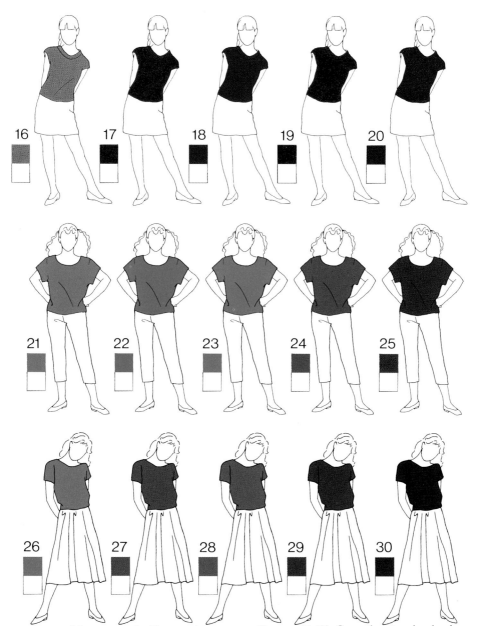

softness of these pastels. The combinations shown in figures 1-6 are classics and appear as favorites every spring. For a newer look, try mixing white with sour yellows or spring greens (figures 7-10).

Summer white usually means cotton—cool, crisp, and easy to care for. A traditional way to use summer white is to mix it with blues and blue greens

(figures 11-15). Once the standard color combination for beach-and-swim-wear, now blue with white is appropriate for day or evening—always cool and neat—the never-fail combination during the long, hot summer. For those days or nights when a little excitement is in order, mix whites with brights (figures 16-30). The effect is dazzling, especially

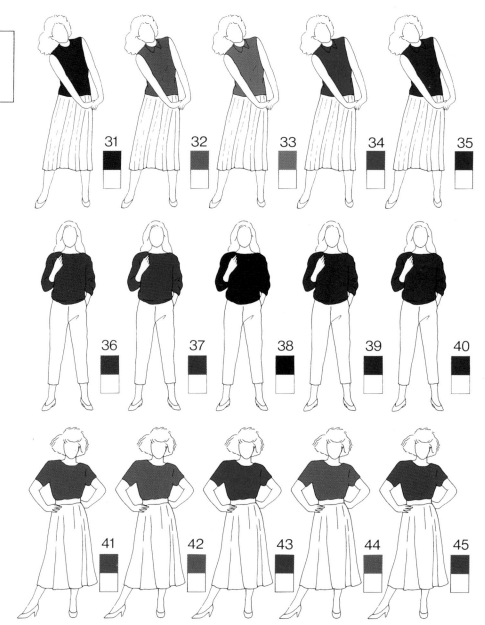

when the color accents used are contrasting brights. Bright and white are easy. Just remember that anything goes.

In figures 31-45, white is combined with dark-toned colors for a different summer look. This kind of mixing is not as popular as white with pastels and brights, but the effect can be refreshingly unusual, especially when silver jewelry and accessories are used as accents.

For a more sophisticated look, combine white with neutrals such as beige or grey (figures 46-59). To look good, the neutral/white combination must be just right—with an emphasis on fabric and shape.

Sometimes the best idea is to go for the ultimate contrast—black and white

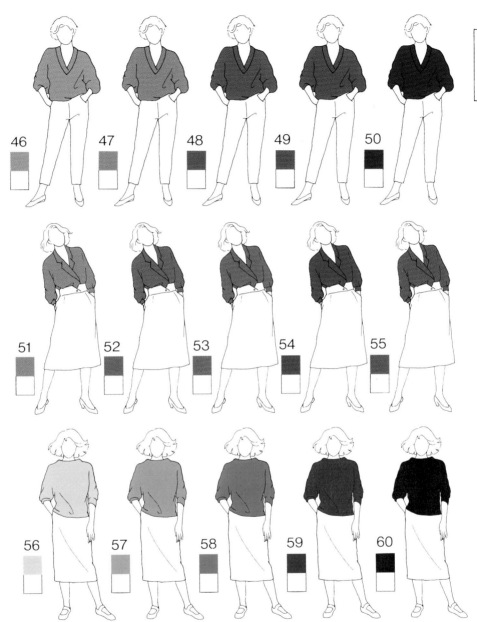

46 47 48 49 50

51 52 53 54 55

56 57 58 59 60

(figure 60). This ever-popular and continually redefined color combination can be serious and sophisticated (like the neutral/white combinations) or jazzy and upbeat (like the color/white mixes). The black/white combination has been immensely popular during the past five years and is already a staple in most wardrobes. Make it new by adding a dash of color—try citron or vermilion. The result will be a maximum of look with a minimum of effort.

White is very effective on its own if the fabric and shape are the focus of the outfit. Be aware, too, of the many shades of white–there are hundreds, as you will discover when beginning to coordinate your spring wardrobe.

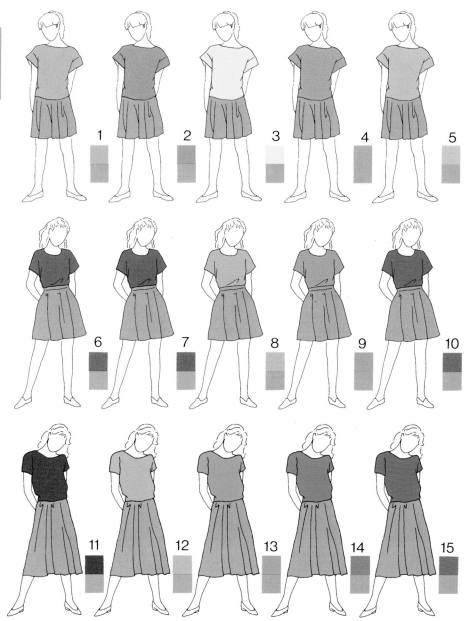

Silver Grey

We tend to consider grey a serious neutral with a minimum of personality. When grey is worn alone—in a flannel business suit, for instance—the words "anonymous" and "boring" come to mind. But, depending on the shade and the way it is combined with other colors, grey can be a romantic pastel or an authoritative neutral.

Silver grey is a cool, refreshing color that acts almost like a pastel. The softness and clarity of this shade encourage the color personality of pastels (figures 1-5) and mid-tone brights (figures 6-15) to shine forth. The pleasant effect of these mixtures is noticeable on a cloudy day when colors take on a

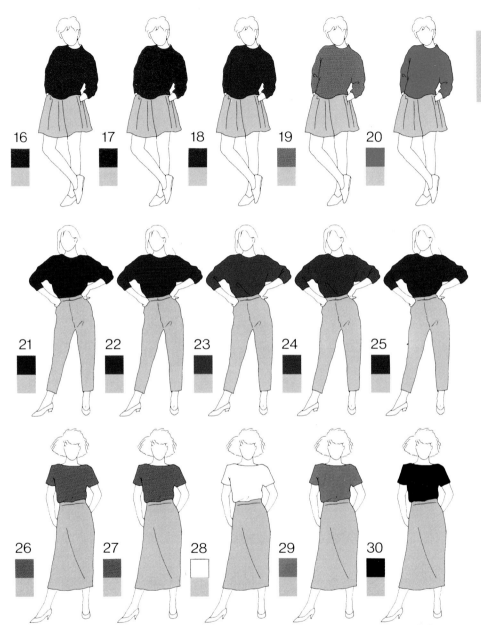

marked intensity and depth in the soft grey light.

Silver grey works best when combined with soft colors, but it can be combined with vivid tones (figures 16-20) if a monotone—black or white—is added to ensure a balance. Bright blue will overwhelm silver grey, but when black or white becomes part of the combination, the effect is one of clean sophistication.

Dark colors such as teal or maroon combine beautifully with silver grey, but the mature, professional look demands perfect grooming from head to toe, as shown in figures 21-29.

Of course, black or white is unfailingly attractive with silver grey.

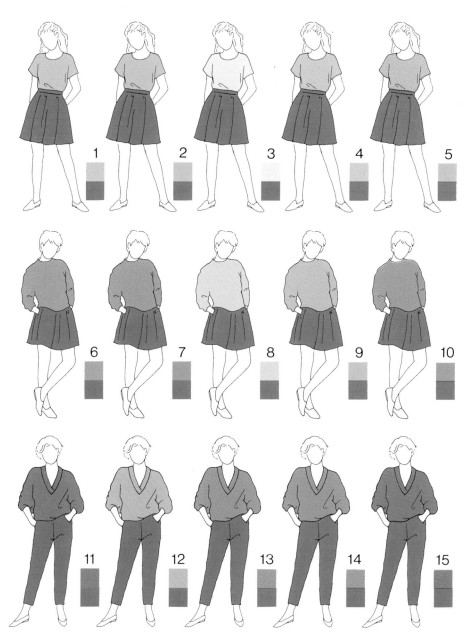

Medium Grey

Medium grey is the most conservative of the grey tones and is probably present in your closet in pants, a skirt, or a jacket.

Once a color that never came out of the office, medium grey is now a fashion color in the active sportswear world. Inventive American designer Norma

Kamali made this grey the season's most fashionable and exciting color in 1980. Combined with soft pastels (figures 1-10), grey evokes images of the dance world. Mixed with brighter pastels (figures 11-15), grey is found in every kind of active sportswear clothing, from shoes to T-shirts.

While the bright pastel/grey combi-

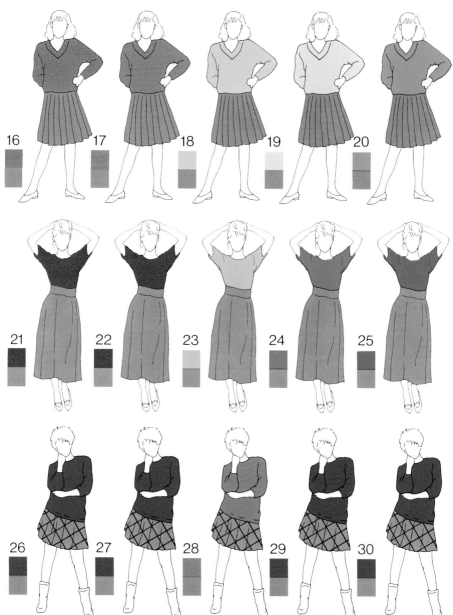

nations can also be used in dressy sportswear separates and dresses, the coupling of grey and slightly sour or unusual brights (figures 16-30) is a much more interesting way to make your trusty grey skirt look new. Try grey with yellow (figure 18), adding touches of white or black for a crisp, urban look. Grey mixed with chartreuse (figure 23) is

contemporary and innovative. Hot pink with grey (figure 22) reflects the influence of Japanese fashion on American taste.

Consider mixing grey with dark or jewel brights to create non-traditional combinations. The soft neutral tone of the grey enhances and accentuates the deep richness of the colors in figures

17

31-45. These slightly unconventional but innovative mixes suggest ways to promote individuality through color. Even as accents, these colors can add personality to an otherwise uniform-like look.

The softest and prettiest grey combinations are shown in figures 46-52. These unusual neutral tones blend attractively with grey to create a soft and sophisticated tonal image.

Grey mixed with other grey, white, or black (figures 56-60) can look harsh and limited without the softening touch of an accent color. Grey with black is unquestionably the favorite fashion combination in Japan; in the U.S., however, this mix is often considered too severe and limited.

18

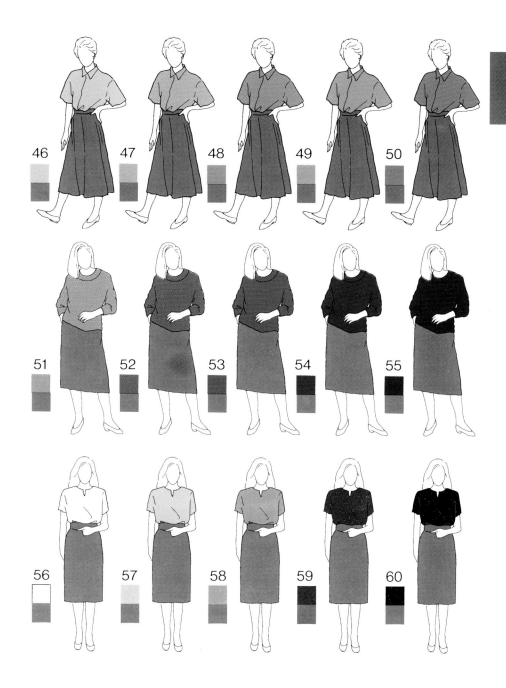

46

47

48

49

50

51

52

53

54

55

56

57

58

59

60

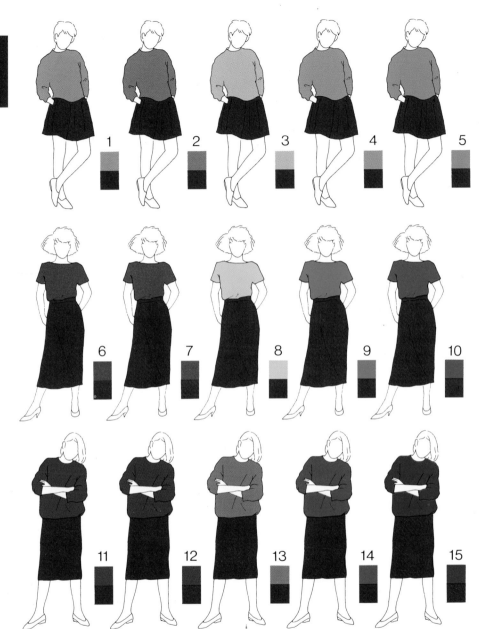

Charcoal Grey

So close to black without being black, charcoal grey is a subtle and provocative color that offers the depth and drama of black without the harshness. When black is too strong, this is the color to choose. Charcoal not only mixes comfortably with brights (figures 1-7), it offers a sophisticated and interesting image when combined with jewel tones (figures 11-15).

For more conventional wardrobe coordinations, combine charcoal with soft neutrals and bright neutrals (figures 16-25). These tonal relationships, subtle in character, offer a wide range of possibilities for color mixing and layering.

Charcoal lends itself to mixing with

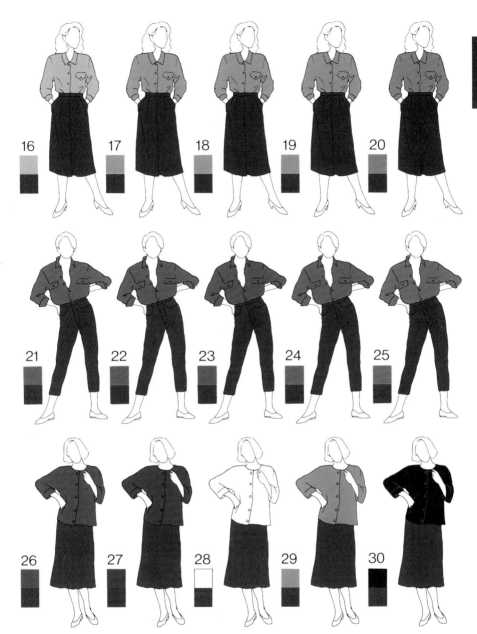

16

17

18

19

20

21

22

23

24

25

26

27

28

29

30

monotones, as well as with other shades
of grey (figures 26-30). To add an appealing dimension to the more subdued
combinations, wear an accessory to
accent one of the brighter neutrals
(figure 21 or figure 24).

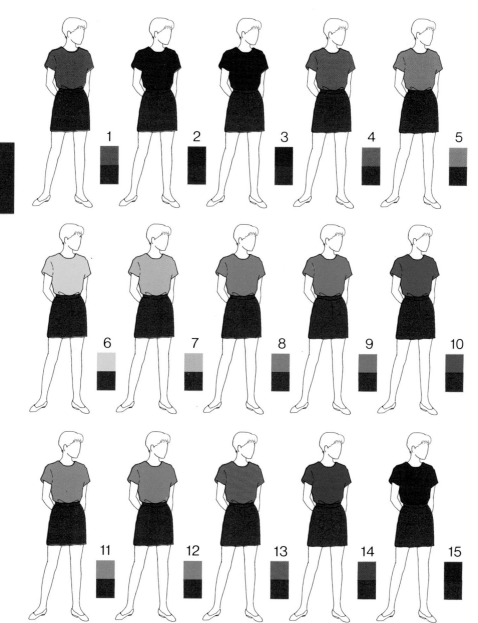

Red

Red is a highly charged, emotional color with universal appeal. It is the first color a baby responds to, making red a popular choice for children's clothes. An advancing color, red can be very high-fashion and is a basic for many designers who sometimes play other colors against its brilliance.

In figures 1-15, red is shown with vivid, high-contrast colors, combinations you often find in casual and active sportswear. The designer Kenzo uses these bold colors to create fresh, vigorous designs that are particularly appealing to contemporary and junior customers.

Figures 16-25 exemplify a young look more often seen in prints than in sepa-

rates. Although white is often added to a combination of, say, pale yellow and red for bright summer look, the brighter colors are much more appealing.

In figures 26-30, the only neutrals that really work with red are off-white (figure 26) and grey (figure 30).

The combinations in figures 31-35 are often used in traditional African prints and can be beautiful when handled correctly. The colors look stunning against a tanned skin.

Red with beige and brown (figures 36-40) can be made more appealing by adding ivory or white. Note how the addition of pattern breaks the intensity of the red.

Dark blues and greens with red

23

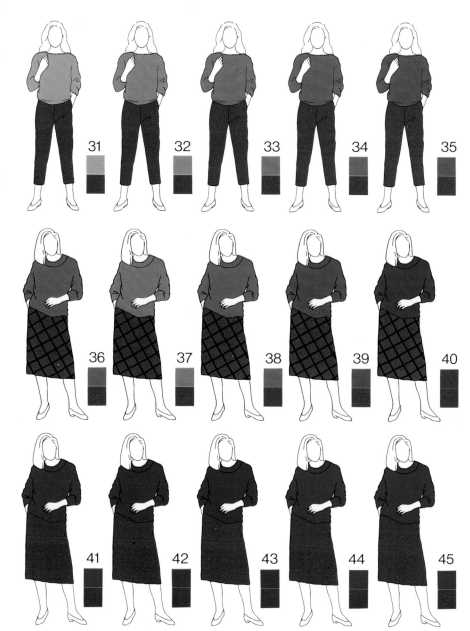

(figures 41-45) have become the cornerstone of preppie dressing and turn up in everything from tartan plaids to combinations of navy blazers and red Shetland sweaters.

When red is worked with khaki and olive (figures 46-50), the resulting combinations are favorites when the safari and military looks become popular

(they always do every few years).

The combinations in figures 51-55 usually only work in a print where other colors are added to soften the cold feeling. Any of the combinations in figures 56-60 are classic and obviously workable. In all of these cases, add white or ivory to soften the combinations and make them basic to any wardrobe.

24

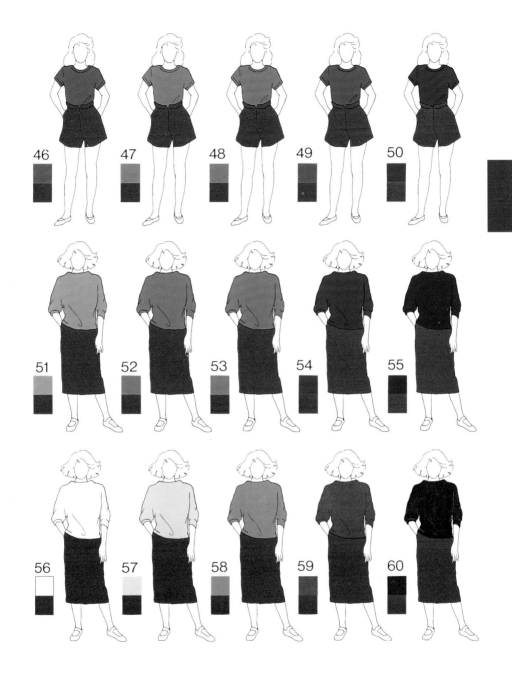

46

47

48

49

50

51

52

53

54

55

56

57

58

59

60

25

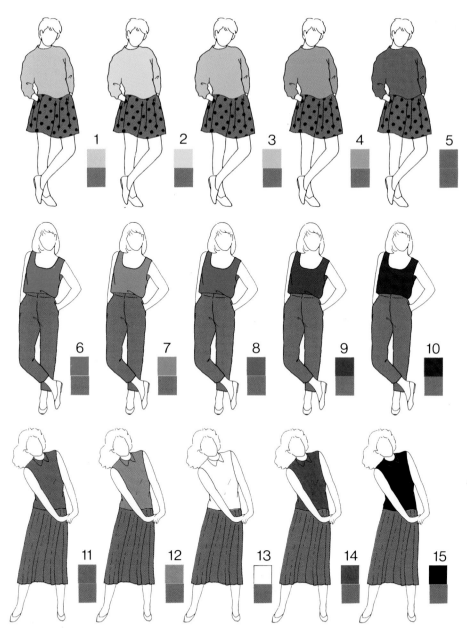

Cherry Pink

Pink is a delicious, feminine color that combines easily with other colors to give a pleasantly young look. In figures 1-5, pink is matched with bright pastels, creating a favorite combination for spring dressing, particularly among teenagers. The ratio of pink to pastel can be fifty-fifty without either color becom-

ing overbearing. With the strong, bright tones shown in figures 6-9, pink would be more effectively used as an accent.

For a more conservative look, combine pink with a beige or a monotone (figures 11-15). For a sharp and sophisticated look that works well for evening dress, match pink with white, grey, or black (figures 13-15).

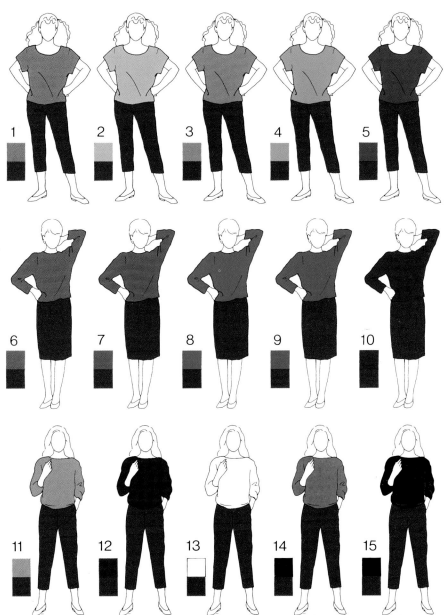

Magenta

Magenta, an intense and emotional color seldom worn by itself, can create a striking statement when mixed with other colors. The rich, tropical shades of orange, gold, khaki, and blue (figures 1-5) create seductive and exotic combinations when mixed with magenta. While these mixes make a sizzling summer and early fall color palette, use magenta as an accent with brown and olive (figures 6-7) for a perfect fall look.

Magenta can, of course, be mixed with the monotones (figures 11-15), but the look is somewhat hard and flat. To appreciate the real value of this color, use it to brighten and enliven other colors, such as purple, gold, and olive.

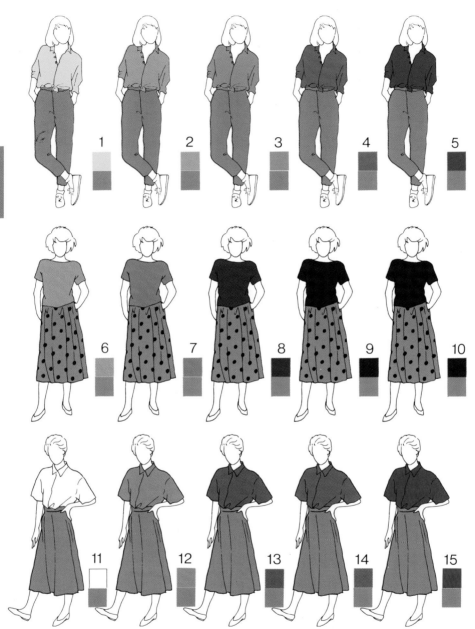

Coral Pink

Coral Pink, a warm, exotic color that could almost be considered a member of the orange family, is reminiscent of summer sunshine, palm trees, and great tans. While it is not as popular a color as cherry pink, coral is an easy mixer that appears with fair regularity, usually in combination with summer yellows and blues (figures 1-5). Coral doesn't have the versatility of a softer pink, but it can work as a nice accent to bring brightness and softness to grey tones (figures 6-8 and 12-15). Keep coral away from purple (figures 9-10)—it kills both colors.

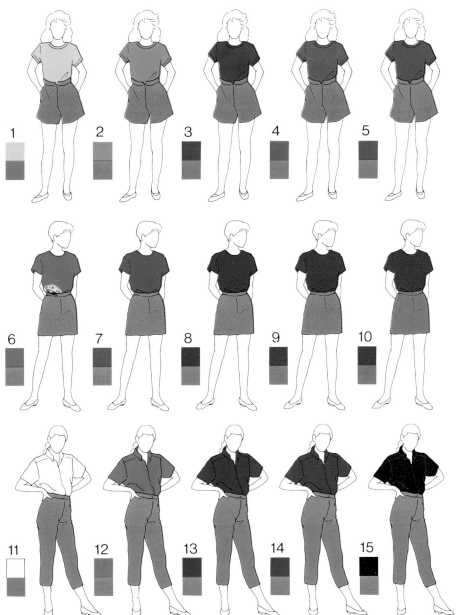

Orange

Orange is a bold, aggressive color that comes into fashion about every twenty years, then disappears from all clothing except uniforms in fast-food chains. During the mid-sixties, it was tremendously popular with purple and lime green in a jarring triumvirate known as "psychedelic colors." Now, twenty years later, orange is again back in fashion. As before, its mates are the bright, acidic colors seen in figures 1-9. These colors are often used by the avant-garde designers from Japan and England to accentuate the boldness of their iconoclastic fashion. As an accent, orange looks easy and natural. On its own, it is suitable only for Halloween attire.

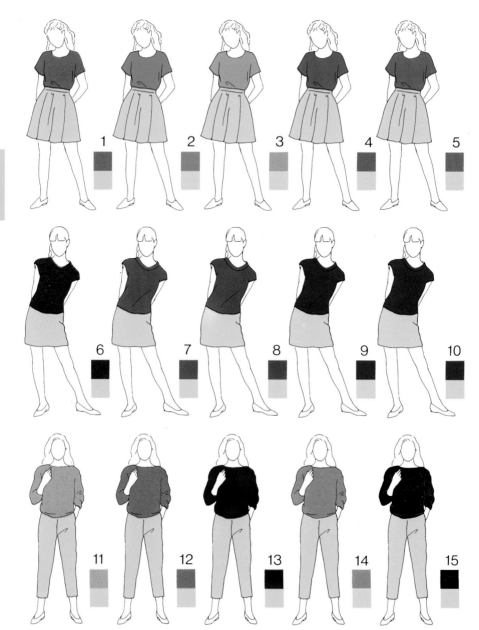

Yellow

Yellow is a color best used in small amounts—by itself, it can be overbearing and oppressive. It is often the color selected for such activities as sailing and skiing because of its high visibility—something most people prefer to avoid in a personal wardrobe.

Yellow will freshen and brighten any

of the medium brights (figures 1-5) or the less-traditional colors in figures 6-10 if added in small amounts as an accessory.

Yellow paired with grey, charcoal, or black (figures 11-15) can be stunning; add white to keep the combination fresh and clean looking. Consider combining yellow with black and white or grey and white for winter woolens.

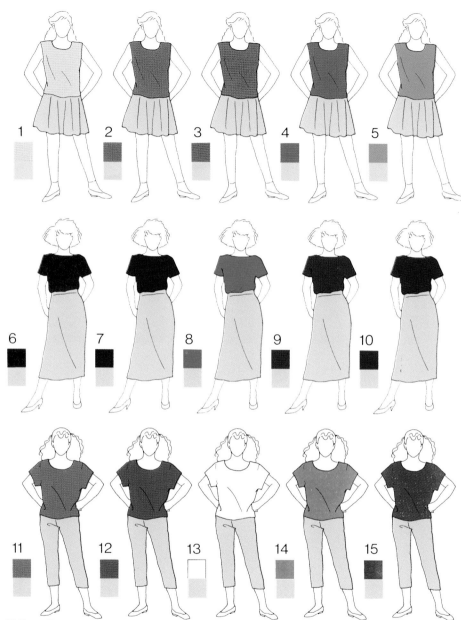

Yellow Green

Yellow green, like orange, is in high fashion strictly for the moment. Because this color will make any skin appear sallow if used in large amounts, combine it with white for freshness or use it as an accent with bright colors (figures 1-5) or jewel tones (figures 6-10). Be sure to keep this color on the bottom as a skirt or pants. At best, yellow green is tricky to use tastefully, but it can be an effective, emotive color when combined with charcoal (figure 15).

Don't buy too much of this color— yellow green will be as "out" next year as it is "in" this year. If you love this color but feel hesitant, perhaps a pair of anklets is the best investment.

31

Mint Green

Mint green, which is not particularly appealing when worn on its own, is surprisingly easy to coordinate with a range of colors—from pastels to autumnal browns, ochers, and wine.

For spring and summer dressing, use mint green as an accent color with light pastels (figures 1-5). With the medium pastel tones (figures 6-10), mint green can balance the pastel and be used as a blouse, skirt, or pants. Adding white will accentuate the freshness of both colors.

In figures 11-15, mint green is tonally balanced with medium bright tones, and the effect is summertime dressing at its best. These very appealing color

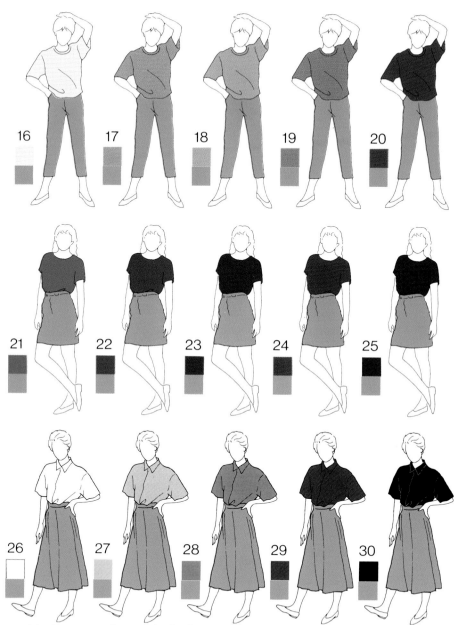

combinations are upbeat and refreshing.

Mint green becomes flat and cold when mixed with off-white, mustard, or brown (figures 16-20). Blues and plums (figures 21-25) are livelier and more workable, but use the mint green mainly as an accent and not the primary color in these combinations. Enhance these mixes by adding silver jewelry, or add white for a clean, modern look.

Turquoise jewelry can be beautiful with black, grey, or white (figures 26-30), but too much mint green will create a hard, aggressive look. Mint green is difficult to wear against the face, so use it in carefully measured amounts in a skirt or in pants.

Malachite

Malachite is particularly good when paired with blues, purples, or magentas. Like mint green, it should not be worn next to the face or in large amounts, but it makes a wonderful accessory color that has the appeal of being unexpected and chic.

Green with pink or peach (figures 1-2) works well for summer sportswear; the malachite and blue mixes (figures 5 and 10) works as well for winter woolens as for summer cottons.

Grey (figure 11) makes the green look harsh and garish, but malachite used with white or black (figures 14-15), with white or colored accents, is original and appealing.

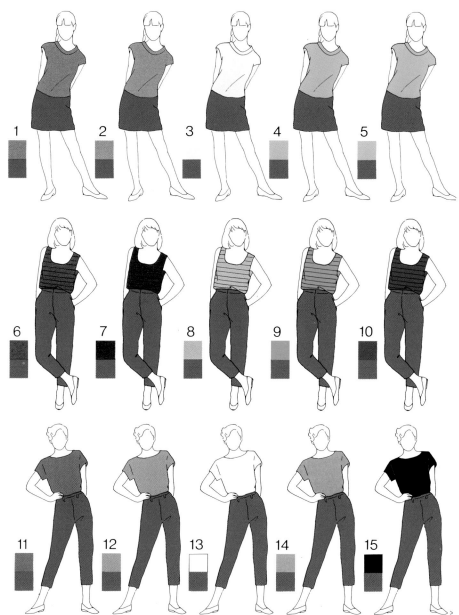

Cobalt Blue

A popular color choice, this highly charged, aggressive color combines effortlessly with other brights (figures 1-10).

The brights in figures 6-10 have similar tonal values as the cobalt and are often referred to as the "cobalt colors." These colors balance one another, but the black accent prevents a flat image and tempers the intensity of these combinations.

The strength of cobalt blue is obvious when it is combined with neutrals, white, and black (figures 11-15). The best combinations are with white (figure 13) and black (figure 15). Cobalt blue works best in a graphic, high-contrast relationship—it overwhelms greys and browns.

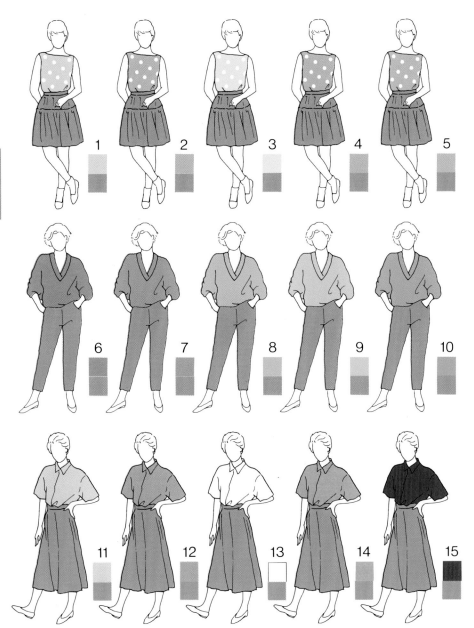

Candy Blue

Candy blue represents the washed-denim look, where the rough-and-ready texture of the denim weave compensates for the flatness of the color.

For denim dressing, this blue goes well with pastels and neutrals, but strong brights tend to overwhelm the paleness of the color.

To balance the receding quality of this pale blue, pick it up with dashes of soft color and an accent of white (figures 1-6). The bright pastels in figures 6-10 also work well in blouses or sweaters with the pale color on the bottom.

With grey, beiges, and white, the blue appears brighter, but these safe combinations are not very interesting.

36

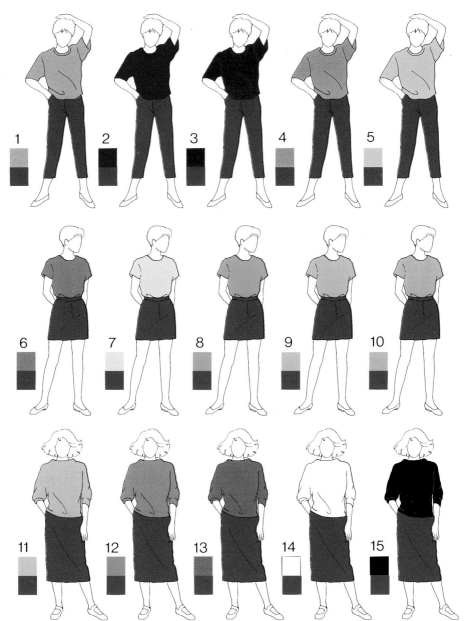

Royal Blue

Royal blue is an easy color to coordinate and is almost foolproof when used as bottoms in skirts and pants. Blouses, T-shirts, or sweaters in warm primaries such as bright red (figure 3) and bright yellow (figure 5) are traditional favorites and look wonderful on a broad spectrum of complexions and ages.

This bright blue accentuates the vibrancy of bright pastels, as well as primaries. In figures 6-10, royal blue works effortlessly from brown through sky blue. Matching royal blue with neutrals (figures 11-13) results in somewhat less effective combinations, but with white and black (figures 14-15), royal achieves a clear and sophisticated look.

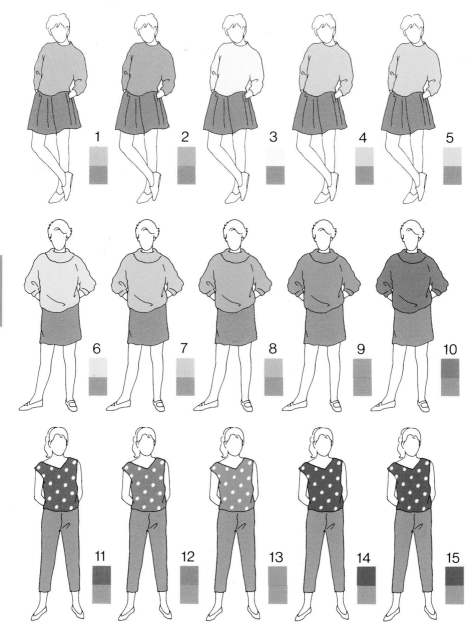

Candy Pink

Candy pink is primarily thought of as a "baby color" for the exclusive use of the young and very young. However limited it might seem, candy pink can be worn with brights to bring unexpected freshness to traditional spring and summer color combinations.

In figures 1-10, candy pink combines easily with other pastels but can also look new when mixed with pale yellow and lime green (figures 6-7). These ten combinations are typical of loungewear and active sportswear looks, whether for dance, aerobics, or the beach.

In figures 11-15, candy pink is paired with other brights and a dash of white. The effect is still fun-in-the-sun, but pink

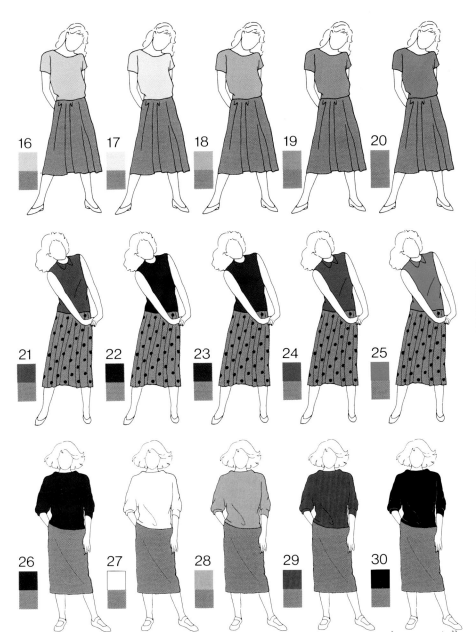

here is slightly unexpected and gives the whole outfit a clean, updated look.

Candy pink paired with neutrals (figures 16-23) can have interesting and effective results when done with a sure and experienced hand, but generally these are combinations to steer clear of. You can quickly see how overbearing the pink becomes. Pink can, of course,

be a marvelous accent color, especially when used with grey (figure 20) or green (figure 25). A little goes a long way, however, so keep the amount small.

In figures 26-30, candy pink combines easily with deep blue, white, grey, or black and keeps these monotones bright and alive. Again, use just a touch to make a point.

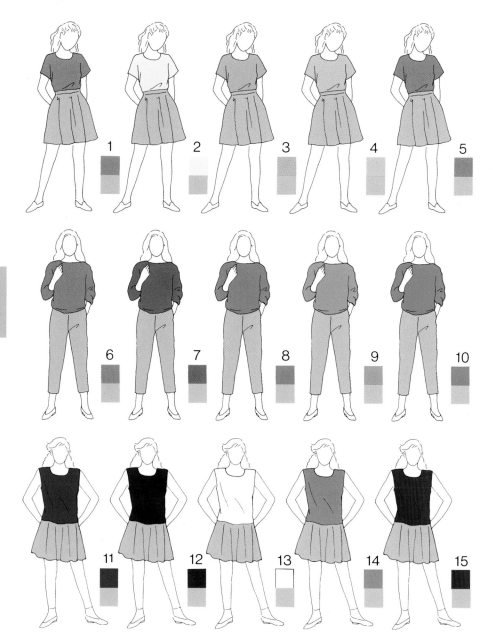

Powder Pink

Unlike other pinks, which project when used with neutrals and monotones, powder pink recedes and allows other colors (figures 7, 12, and 15) to dominate. Powder pink can be used in large amounts because it operates almost as an off-white or light grey. This is the pink to use if you are looking for an urban, dressy look with a bit of dash.

We expect powder pink to be paired with pastels (figures 1-5), but it is much more effective when used with blues (figures 6-10).

Powder pink combined with dark blue (figure 11) and brown (figure 12) is chic and appealing and would work for any season by adding cream or ivory.

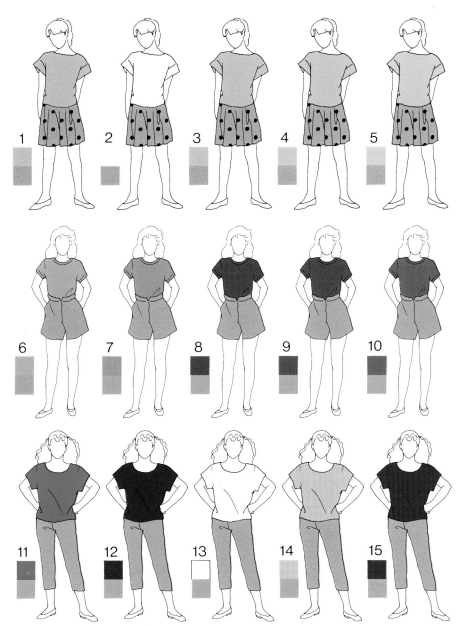

Peach

Peach emphasizes the healthy glow of a good tan, so avoid this color if your complexion is fair (even if only during the winter months when most complexions tend to be sallow—peach will only accentuate this quality).

For easy summer combinations, pair peach with pastels (figures 1-5) and add a touch of black for smartness.

Use peach with earth tones (figures 6-9) to give beiges and greys a fresh aspect.

Peach tends to sap blue and green (figures 10-12) of their appealing qualities. Even when used sparingly in such combinations, the peach will dominate, so avoid the whole idea.

41

Cream

Cream, an easy mixer and a good staple, is not as bright and demanding as yellow, yet projects a warm image when combined with other colors.

When mixed with pastels (figures 1-5), cream creates pleasant spring combinations. Used in addition to, or instead of, white in a print, cream softens the look and produces a warm, sophisticated effect.

With bright pastels (figures 6-10), use cream as you would a bright yellow—as an accent. Also use cream as an accent with brights (figures 11-15); although there is nothing wrong with the cream/bright combinations, they are the least appealing of all these mixes.

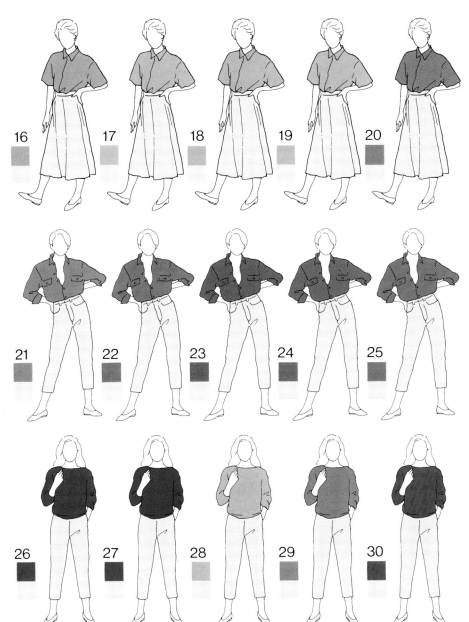

Cream mixes nicely, however, with all of the greys, browns, and natural hues shown in figures 16-30. While the bright tones make cream seem washed out, the naturals allow it to perform its best function—bringing warmth and softness to the combination. Whether cream is paired with soft naturals (figures 16-20), or the darker naturals (figures 21-30), the result is appealing and easy to understand.

For a nice effect when mixing cream with other natural colors, use a natural, unrefined fiber—such as linen, silk, wool, or cotton—that has been slubbed or otherwise treated to bring out the surface character of the material.

Spring Yellow

For many years, spring yellow has been grouped with other pastels and never considered an important color on its own. In recent years, however, it has slowly but definitely emerged as a valued fashion color epitomizing the importance of unusual colors in the fashion world of the eighties.

Spring yellow combines easily with the pastels in figures 1-5. To create a soft yet sophisticated impression, use these combinations in crisp spring linens. When spring yellow is paired with other pastels (figures 6-10), the impression is different—the pale yellow brings a fresh, modern look to these tones. A pair of yellow pants or a large over-

44

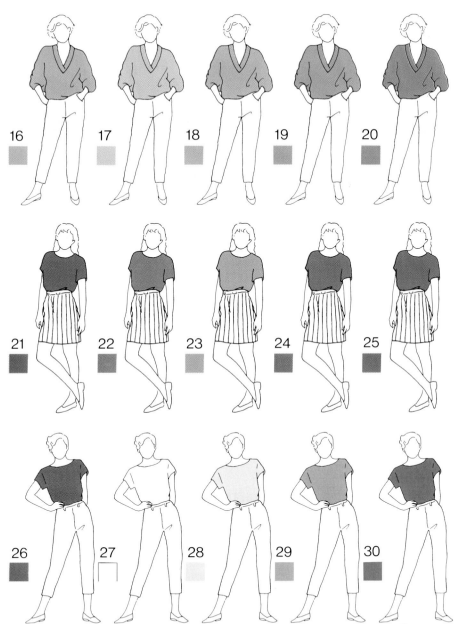

shirt can act as an accessory and make a fashion statement. In the same way, spring yellow can be used with brights (figures 11-15). While this yellow is fine with reds and other yellows, it becomes much more special when combined with greens, blues, and purples. If you add white with magenta accents, the image is almost fauvist.

In figures 16-26, spring yellow is mixed with naturals. While it combines very well with greys, this color is too cool to mix well with the browns.

In figures 27-30, spring yellow is seen with white and cool greys. When black, charcoal, or a bright purple or blue is added here, the effect is as striking as it is new.

Spring Green

Spring green works wonderfully with medium brights if it is kept away from the face.

Spring green pairs comfortably with pastels (figures 1-5) and brings a fresh look to colors that could otherwise be considered maudlin. The black accent suggests a very contemporary look that prevails in young sportswear in Japanese, European, and American fashions.

In the spring green and medium bright combinations (figures 6-10), the softness of the brights balances with the green and allows it to be worn in large amounts in prints or skirts.

The combinations in figures 11-15 are too harsh and should be avoided.

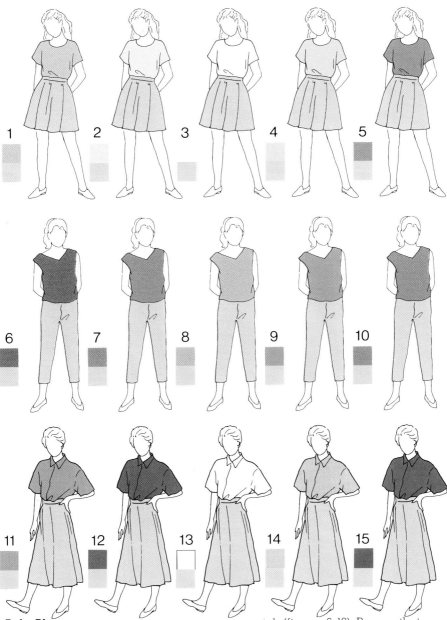

Baby Blue

This delicate, unpretentious color is easy to coordinate when its companion pieces blend tonally with the blue. In figures 1-5, baby blue is mixed with equally delicate pastels, creating tonal blends that could be beautiful in wool or lightweight linen.

Baby blue also works with bright pastels (figures 6-10). Beware that any color brighter than these will cause the already receding blue tone to almost disappear.

Mixed with soft neutrals and white (figures 11-15), the blue becomes stronger and brighter. To enhance any of these fresh combinations, add accessories in a warm peach or soft beige.

47

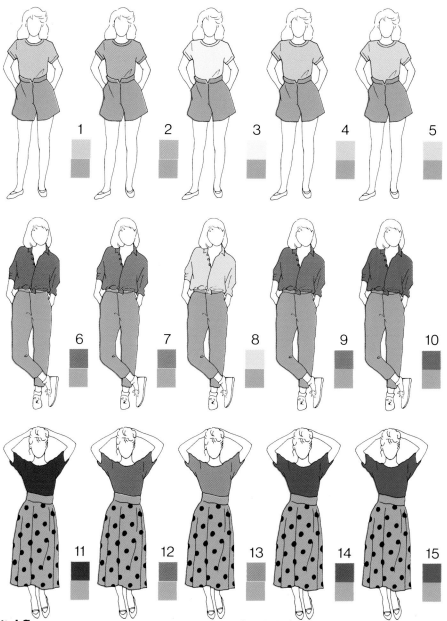

Hospital Green

While it is an enormously popular clothing color in Japan and some other Asian countries, in the United States hospital green has always been either a rather esoteric fashion color or a very common color closely associated with institutional uniforms.

This pale green looks best when mixed with the medium brights (figures 6-9) where it is weighted equally. In most other combinations, the green is intrusive to the point of dominating the other colors.

Even as an accent, hospital green contributes very little to another color. For this reason, you may want to forget this color entirely and go on to aqua or malachite green.

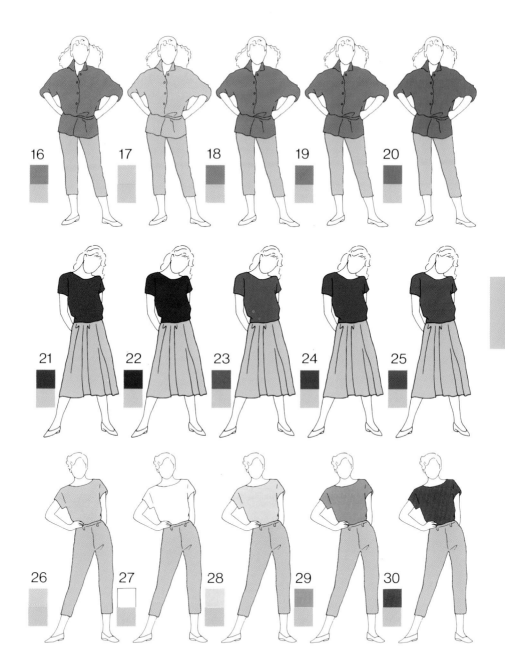

16

17

18

19

20

21

22

23

24

25

26

27

28

29

30

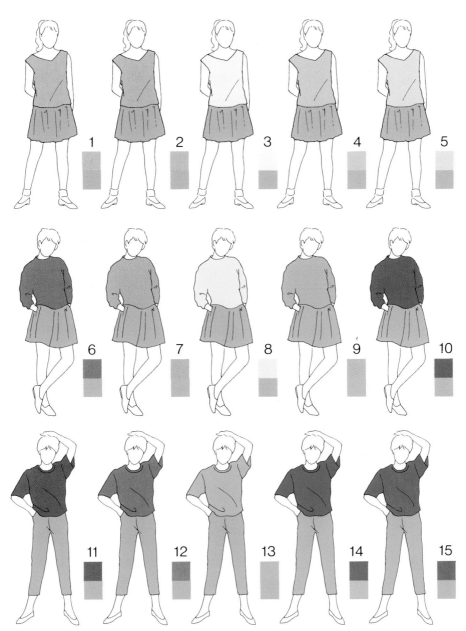

Aqua

Aqua is an enormously popular sportswear color that can be worn easily by people of any age and any coloring.

With pastels (figures 1-5), aqua is an easy mixer. Add white for brightness or black for sophistication; any combination works. Aqua is perfectly balanced with bright pastels (figures 6-10). For a

strikingly bright and sporty effect, mix colors by color-blocking—combine aqua pants with a yellow T-shirt (figure 8) and a purple jacket (figure 10).

When paired with medium brights (figures 11-15), aqua recedes and can act as an anchor for the bright tones.

Used with neutrals (figures 16-20), aqua projects and can be very flattering

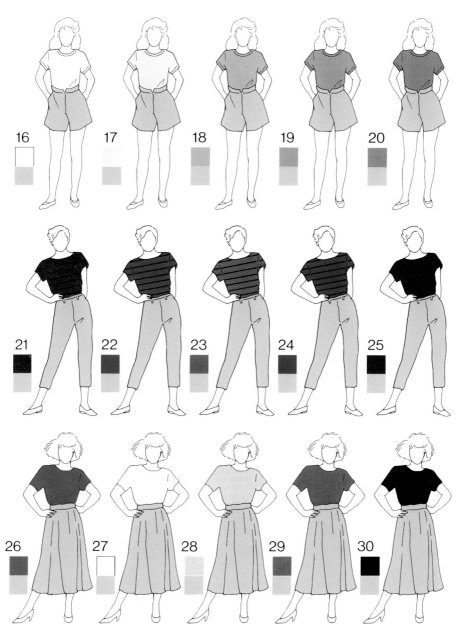

in lesser proportion—as a cardigan sweater or a print—to the neutral. These color combinations, especially when accented with coral or warm pink, are very attractive on tanned or dark complexions.

Aqua is least successful when mixed with bright primary colors (red and blue in figures 21-22) or with greys and black (figures 26-30). In these cases, aqua works well only as an accent.

Used with browns, aqua takes on an appealing, exotic green cast and makes the brown appear warm. This combination can be a bit tricky, but consider using natural, woven browns with turquoise jewelry for an unusual yet lovely look.

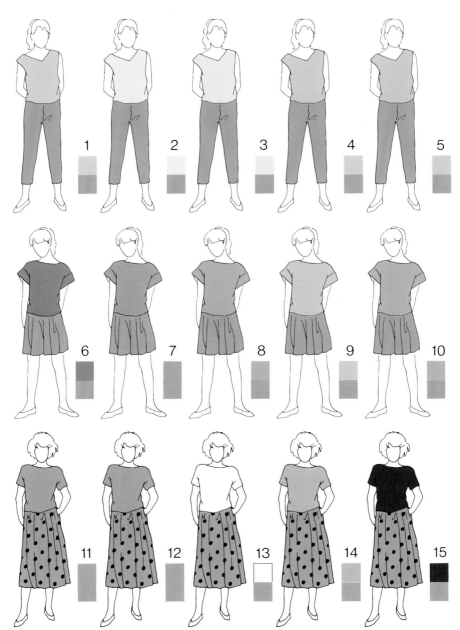

Lavender Blue

Cool, dusky lavender blue is a wonderful mixer that should be used only in bottoms or as an accent color.

With white and any medium pastel (figures 1-5), the lavender acts like blue. Color-block this color with bright pastels (figures 6-10) for a unique look. Paired with spring green, lavender blue calls out for yellow accents.

With neutrals (figures 11-12), use lavender blue only as an accent. For a chic look, add a dash of beige and black to lavender blue. With white (figure 13), this lavender leaves a fresh, clean image. Lavender always brightens grey or black (figures 14-15).

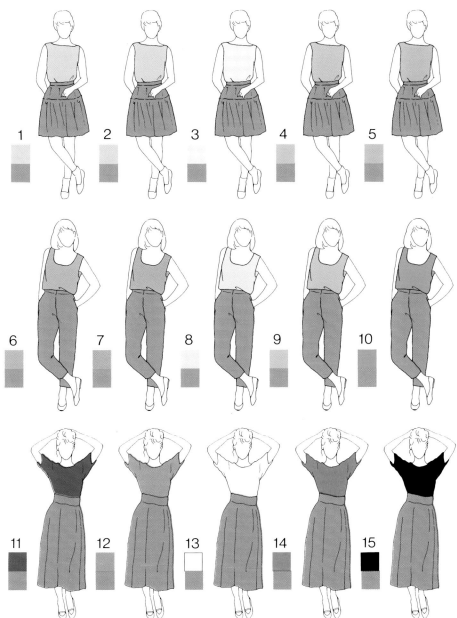

Lavender

Lavender looks good with blond or white hair but tends to make golden or dark complexions appear sallow and washed out.

With pastels (figures 1-5), lavender acts almost as a neutral—much as grey does—by heightening the tones of the pastels and keeping them from becoming sickly sweet.

When mixed with medium brights (figures 6-10), lavender creates a young, exciting sportswear look—orange, yellow, green, and lavender mix easily here.

Use discretion when pairing lavender with purple, grey, white, or black (figures 11-15)—these combinations are rather dark and flat.

53

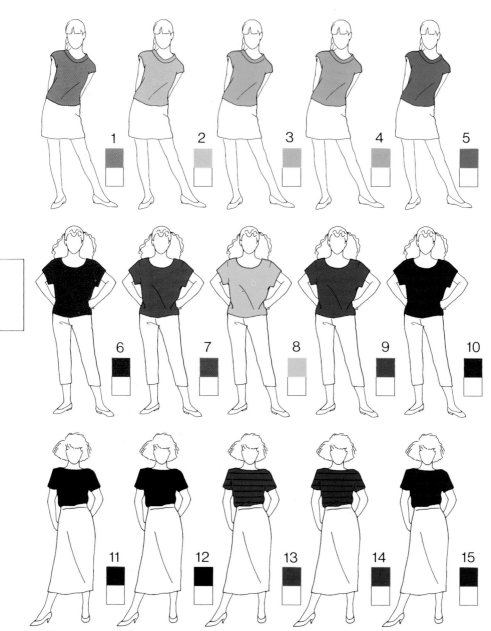

Off-White

This soft, glowing color accentuates the warmth in its companion colors and mixes best with neutrals and monotones. Off-white, when used in winter woolens, is called "winter white."

Coupling off-white with bright pastels (figures 1-5) produces a warmer and softer image than expected with pastels and white.

When mixed with dark brights (figures 5-10), off-white can create some tricky combinations because the bright brights give the off-white a slightly soiled appearance. If mixed correctly, however, the dark pastels balance the off-white with surprising results.

Off-white complements the browns,

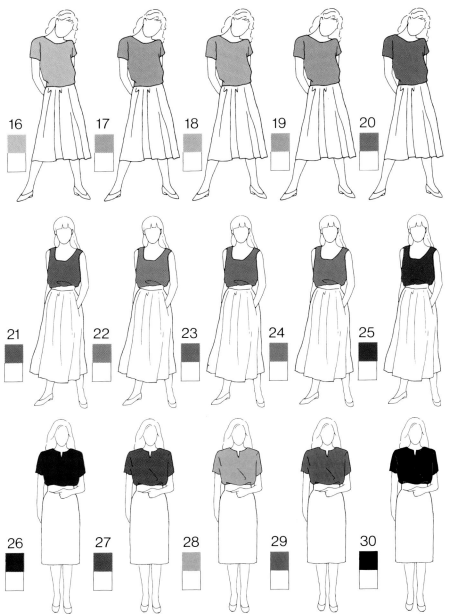

● オフホワイト

charcoal, and deep blue accented with black (figures 11-15) and creates a cool, neat summer look. Ivory or gold jewelry adds polish.

With pale neutrals and the beiges in figures 16-20, off-white is a natural and achieves a soft, sophisticated look no matter how it's used—in equal proportions or as an entire off-white en-

semble accented by the neutrals.

Stronger neutrals (figures 21-25) are just as effective and contrast with off-white, making it appear sharper and brighter. Again, gold jewelry balances the relationship and makes it work.

Used in any ratio, off-white softens the starkness of the monotones in figures 26-30.

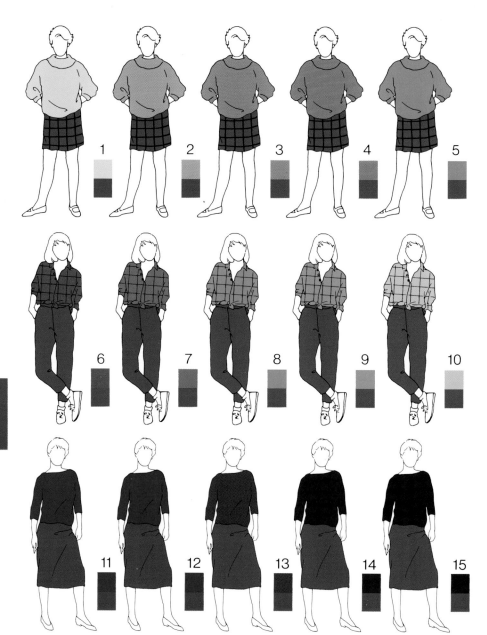

Dark Red

Dark red is a rich, vibrant color that tends to upstage many of the colors it is combined with. Like its close relative, magenta, dark red can bring a dreary outfit to life when used wisely and well.

Overwhelming on its own, this red mixes naturally with neutrals and dark jewel tones. It favors an autumn mood

and takes easily to woolens and textured weaves. The dark red and bright combinations (figures 1-10) are jarring to the eye and should be avoided.

Dark red mixed with the dark jewel tones of purple, blue, or green (figures 11-14), on the other hand, makes a beautiful, well-balanced combination rich in coloring.

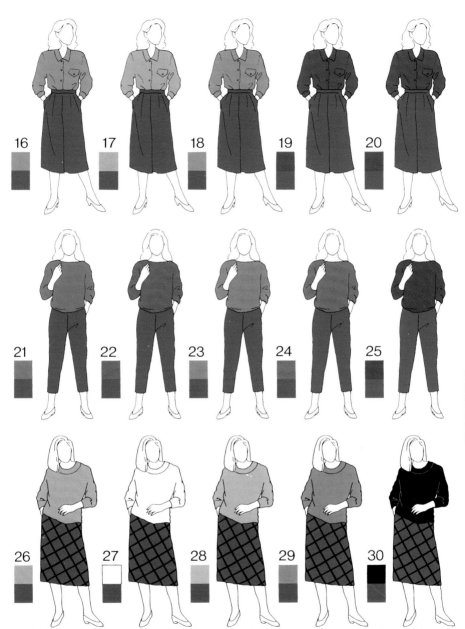

Dark red works equally well with ocher and dark green tones (figures 16-20). These are slightly unusual combinations for the fall season, but consider these colors if you are seeking a new direction.

While the combinations shown in figures 21-25 are not as difficult as the dark red and bright mixes, the flatness of the dusty colors causes the red to overwhelm the softer colors. Instead of blending, the dark red screams and becomes brash and glaring.

Dark red with white (figure 27) has limited appeal and wastes both colors. Dark red and black (figures 30) balance well; for a sophisticated look, use the red as an accent to the black.

Sepia

Sepia is less emphatic than black, charcoal, and navy; otherwise, this dark chocolate brown could almost be considered a basic color. Sepia can, however, help rework your blouses and sweaters when accessories are used to keep the coordination tight. A quick glance over figures 1-30 show the in-

teresting potential of sepia when used in new ways. Consider pairing metallic-colored shoes—copper, bronze, or gold—to add another tonal and textural dimension to the sepia combinations.

In figures 1-15, sepia creates unexpected, intriguing mixes when combined with three tones of brights. The sepia, though dark in tone, has a

58

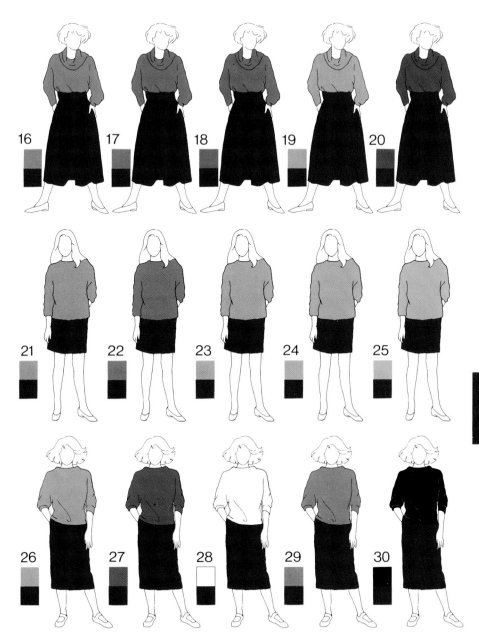

warmth that brings out the vividness of the bright colors. Altogether, there is not a bad combination on the page.

In figures 21-25, dusty tones of rose, celadon, and blue mix gracefully with the sepia to create provocative combinations. These color mixes are expected for fall dressing; they could also be appropriate for summer in natural linen.

Consider wearing silver and turquoise jewelry with these combinations, because soft adobe tones work well with American Indian jewelry.

Sepia mixed with grey, off-white or black (figures 26-30) makes the least attractive combinations. Although passable, these combinations lack the interest and appeal of the earlier colorations.

Brown Gold

Brown gold is more often combined with brights (figures 1-5 and 11-12) than with predictable neutrals (figures 6-10).

Primarily an accent color, a little brown gold goes a long way, so use it prudently. On its own, it can quickly overwhelm even the boldest color. To let this color do its best work, mix it into a plaid or a tweed, where it will enliven winter woolens.

Keep this color away from the face because it will wash out most complexions, but consider using it instead of black in leather shoes, gloves, or a handbag, where the brown gold acquires a rich, luxurious character.

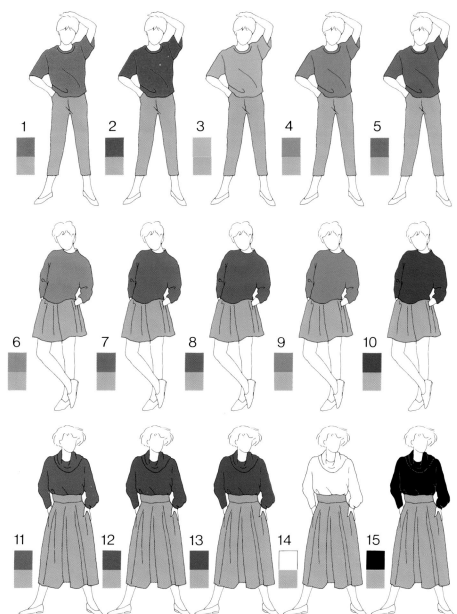

Mustard

Mustard, much misused and maligned, can be an innovative accent color if treated carefully. Some guidelines: Use it with caution and away from the face; use it in an interesting texture; use a yellow mustard rather than a green, or the mustard will appear dirty.

Avoid mustard with brights (figures 1-4)—too brash. The jewel tones (figures 5-13) have too much mustard, but in a balanced relationship the combination would be exciting and new.

Mustard and winter white (figure 14) will work for fall woolens and spring linens. Worn with gold jewelry, mustard and black (figure 15) is a favorite combination for designer sportswear.

Olive Green

Like purple, olive green moves to the forefront every few years as the "color of the season." Though most people have strong opinions on how they look in olive green, this color combines easily with both brights and earth colors and actually can be worn in varying amounts by nearly everyone.

The olive/bright mixes in figures 1-15 are favorites of the European sportswear designers and often turn up in the casual sports separates imported into the United States for a "fashion" summer sportswear look. Consider these combinations for fall dressing as well; they are far from traditional in woolens but just might provide the spark

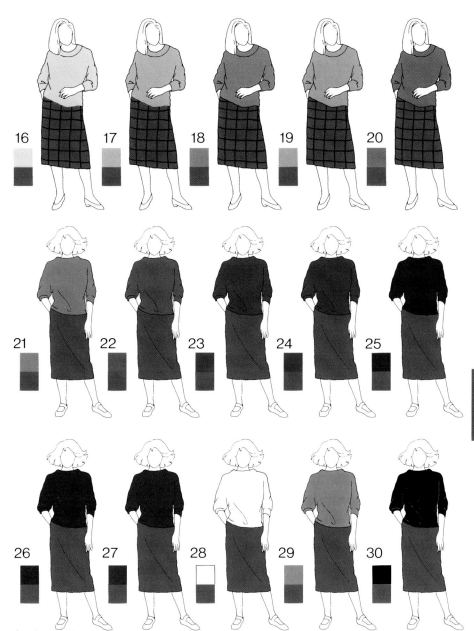

of individuality your wardrobe needs.

In figures 16-20, olive is combined with soft neutrals, and an accent of black gives each of the combinations an added dimension. These are traditional men's wear combinations.

In figures 21-27, jewel tones are mixed with the olive for a classic look that has more depth and interest than

the neutral combinations. While these colors are often used for winter woolens, consider mixing white, pale yellow, or ivory with these colors for summer linens.

Olive with black (figure 30) is a popular and sophisticated combination—if it seems too dark, brighten it up with gold or dark red.

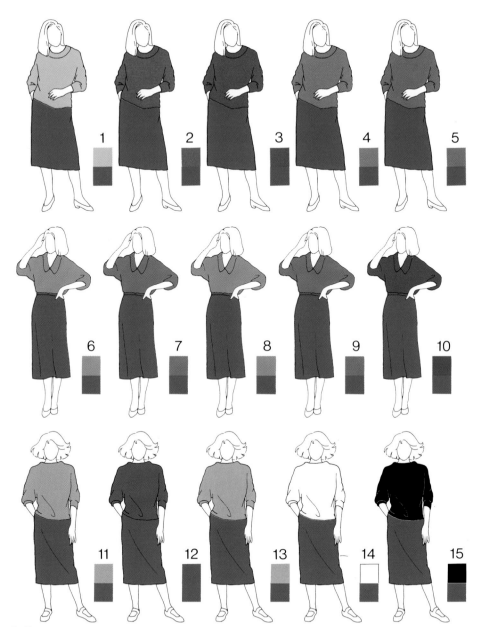

Bottle Green

Bottle green creates an unmistakable autumn look when combined with both brights and neutrals. An unusual and versatile green, it complements all colorings and looks wonderfully rich in fabrics as varied as poplins and nubby woolens. We don't often see bottle green used with brights in such bold

proportions as shown in figures 1-5. In plaids, tweeds, and yarn dyes, however, these combinations are bright but classic.

Bottle green is a brighter, newer tone than forest green and encourages warmth from brown tones (figures 6-10).

The combinations shown in figures 11-15 represent an easy way to update grey or black basics.

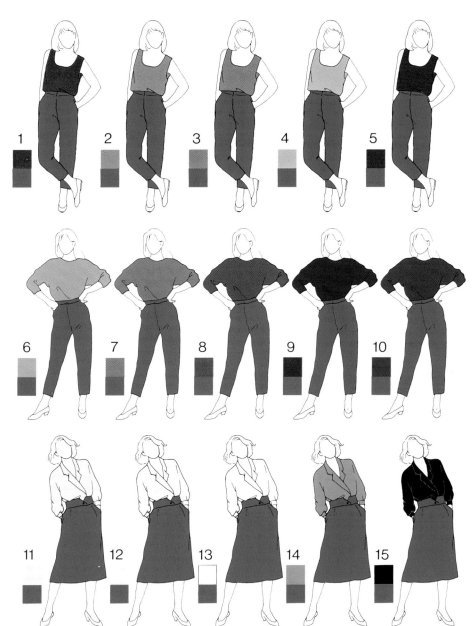

Teal Green

This exotic color can be combined with many colors to add a new dimension to your wardrobe. Like bottle green, teal can be worn by almost any complexion and combines easily with brights, browns, and neutrals.

Mixed with brights (figures 1-5), teal creates a "winter bright" look, made

famous by Kenzo, who begins his winter palette with teal and works to yellow, blue, and pink.

A vibrant, adult color, teal can overwhelm white and light grey (figures 14-15) but looks nice with pale pink (figure 11) and cream (figure 13) when used sparingly. With black (figure 15), teal is very graphic and uptown.

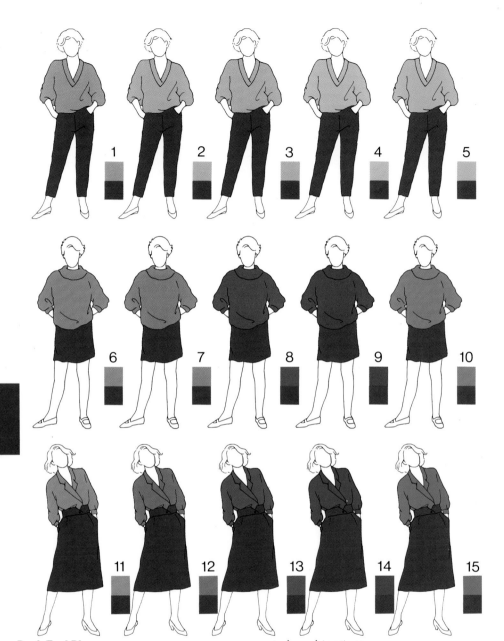

Dark Teal Blue

A deep, seductive color with a tremendous range of uses, dark teal blue can be used as anything from a basic to a high-fashion color.

In figures 1-5, dark teal mixes with dusty pastel tones and takes the place of the expected navy denim for casual dressing, creating distinctive, sophisti-cated combinations.

Dark teal is well-suited to the medium brights in figures 6-10, where the deep blue-green tone of the teal enhances the rich vibrancy of the other colors. The dark brights in figures 11-15 mix tonally with teal and merge to create a single color image appropriate for chic fall dressing.

In figures 16-25, dark teal changes from a recessive color to an advancing color. Mixed with soft neutrals (figures 16-20), dark teal is subdued but effective, and the combinations suggest soft knit shapes—the perfect way to wear these unusual but enticing colors.

Tonally related to dark teal, the darker neutrals in figures 21-25 combine easily with the teal. These mixes call for the right accessories—to avoid a bleak, flat image, for example, introduce jewelry in warm metallic tones.

Dark teal is acceptable with dark colors (grey and black in figures 26-30) and is probably best used with black, where the contrast shows teal's depth and intensity.

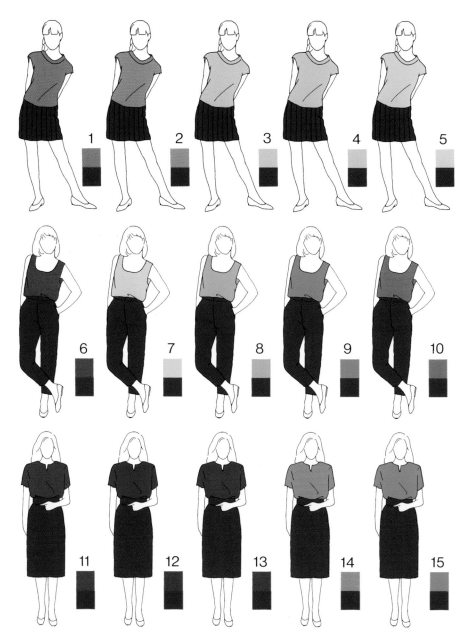

Prussian Blue

This cool, dark blue from the navy and indigo family has a hard cleanness that allows it to mix easily with both neutrals and brights, although the latter mixes are probably less interesting. Prussian blue and brights (figures 1-10) make perfectly acceptable, if conventional, combinations, but the blue takes on an institutional, almost uniformed look.

The more unusual magenta and ocher tones (figures 11-15) enhance the very deep hue of the prussian blue and encourage it to be the very interesting color it is.

The soft, warm neutral tones (figures 16-20) work to the advantage of the blue, showing the depth and richness of the

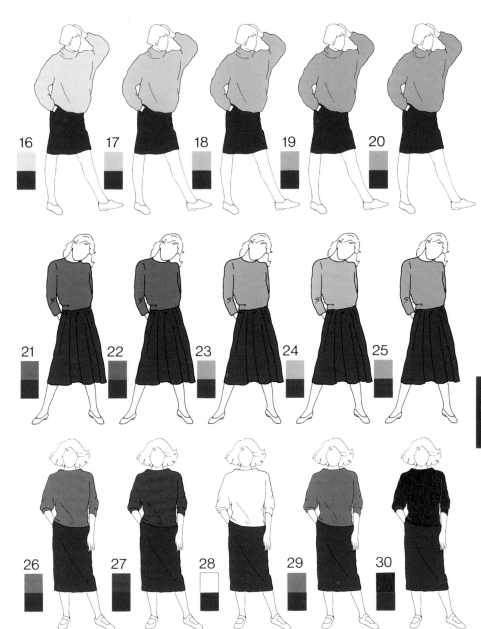

color to good advantage. There is a slight green cast to prussian blue, and it comes out nicely when mixed with warm greys and beiges.

Prussian blue mixed with medium neutrals (figures 21-25) creates conventional combinations suitable for career dressing. Instead of navy, consider using this shade of blue—it tends to mix

with available neutrals in a slightly different way. The effect is richer, especially with silver jewelry as an accessory.

When combined with the flat colors in the grey, white, and black range (figures 26-30), the prussian blue loses its smoothness. The beautiful blue-green tone flattens, and the prevailing color image becomes hard and cold.

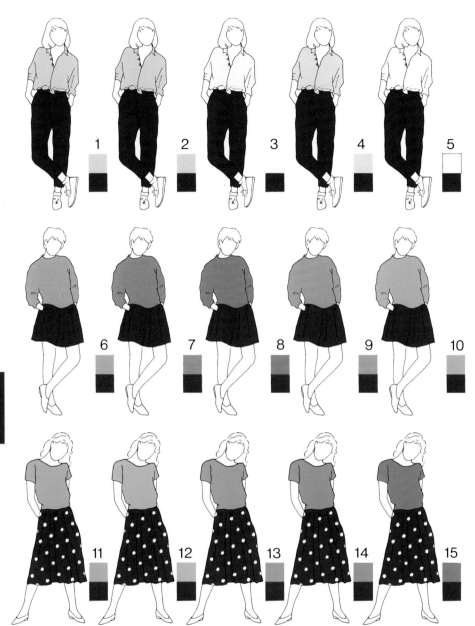

Bright Navy

Like black, bright navy is a basic in most wardrobes and works equally well as a top or a bottom color. It is complementary to most complexions, is staid without having black's severity, works with a broad spectrum of colors, and can have a diversity of personalities—from a tailored silk suit to Levi's 501 jeans.

Light and bright pastels (figures 1-10) as sweaters, T-shirts, and blouses are easy mixers with bright navy jeans. Entire retail empires such as The Gap have been built on this universally popular and distinctively American look.

Bright navy and medium greens and blues (figures 11-15) still mix easily, but note the addition of white on the blue

here. Dark blue and white in a rayon fabric that has both drape and body consciousness can give you a fresh, slightly sophisticated look that is perfect for spring and summer.

The primary and bright navy combinations (figures 16-30) best illustrate the versatility of this color. These active sportswear and casual wear mixes can be worn by anyone, irrespective of age, profession, or gender.

Bright navy and earth tones (figures 31-40) combine well because they are tonally related. These fall colors are particularly effective in sleek wool gabardine. The pumpkin color in figure 37 is surprisingly nice and gives a fresh aspect to the bright blue.

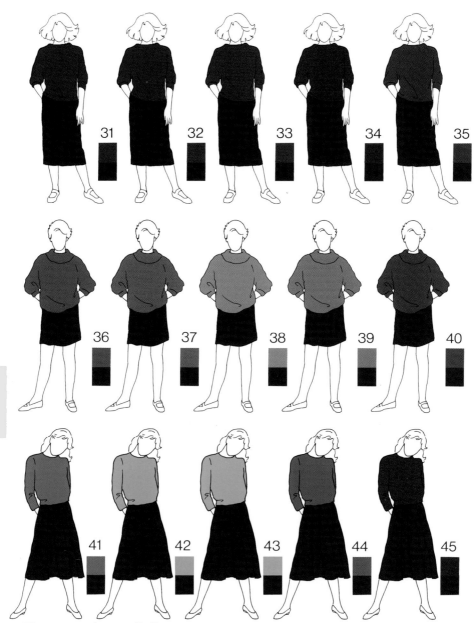

The mixes in figures 41-45 can make the navy in your closet look new and interesting. The dark blue and purple combination in figure 45 is especially innovative and rather unexpected.

Bright navy and the various shades of soft beige, moss, ocher, and grey (figures 46-58), while not wildly exciting, are highly acceptable coordinations.

The navy and white in figure 58 is a perennial favorite for spring dressing. Many designers traditionally put their best fall silhouettes into lightweight navy and white wools for spring for a look that never goes out of style.

Navy and black (figure 60) is a popular combination with Japanese designers but is generally too dark and heavy for American tastes.

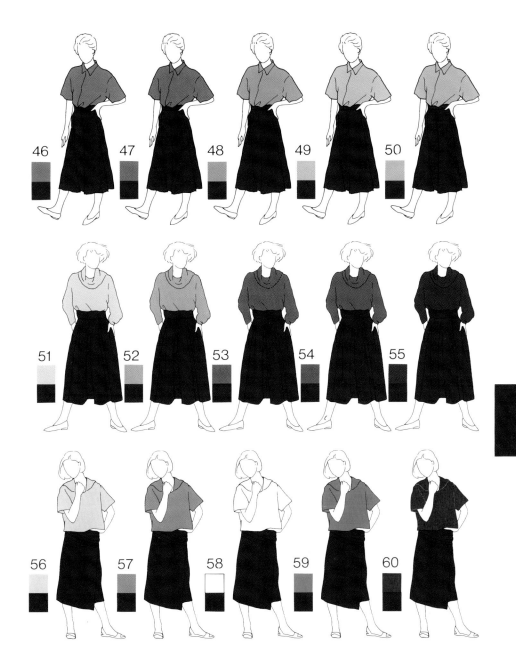

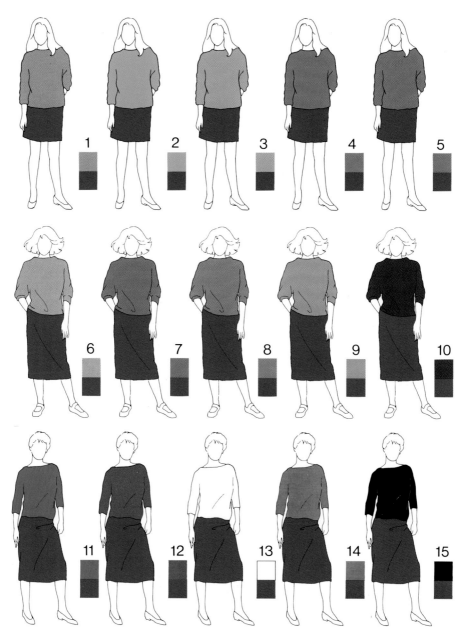

Purple

It is an essential accent color, an important coordinating color, and every four years will surely emerge as "the color of the season." Once regarded as difficult to combine with others and to wear, it is now used with bright colors (figures 1-5) by most designers to create advanced looks.

For a conservative, classic look, team purple with greys, beiges, and moss greens (figures 5-7) in fall woolens.

Purple combined with teal green, claret, black, and grey (figures 11-15) harkens back to royal origins, creating the dramatic, sophisticated jewel tones that are classic fall and holiday season combinations.

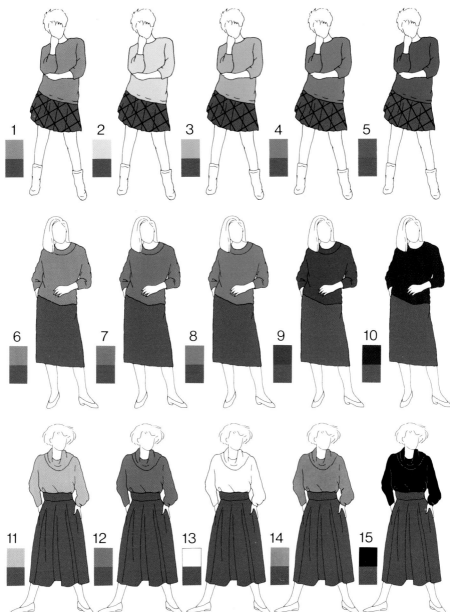

Wine

Like purple, magenta, and mahogany, wine is best used in small measures as a trim, a print, or an accessory. In large doses, this color creates more problems than it solves.

Mixed with a variety of pop-brights (figures 1-5), wine works well only in figures 4 and 5, where the black accent

helps unite the main colors.

Wine with umber and olive (figures 6-10) does not mix easily unless the wine is used as a contrast; wine does balance, however, with the malachite and purple tones.

Wine and off-white, the various shades of grey, and black (figures 11-15) are all tastefully safe combinations.

Beige Grey

Beige grey is a neutral that should be a basic component in every wardrobe for year-round wear. While this color can be mixed with brights for spring and summer, beige grey is most at home when combined with dark brights and earth tones.

The real beauty of a neutral such as beige grey is that it accentuates the colors it is combined with. The dark brights in figures 11-15 show up as rich, illuminated colors that are appropriate for any time of year.

Figures 16-30 show a wide range of colors, from creamy beige to black, combined with beige grey—every combination shows this color's versatil-

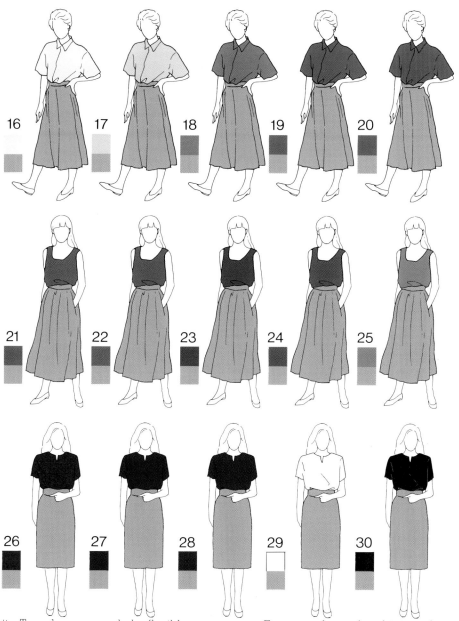

ity. To make your wardrobe flexible, invest in beige grey in several different shapes, including a blazer and a basic straight skirt or trousers. Consider fabrics of various weights—poplin for summer, for example, and wool or cotton and wool gabardine for fall. Wear these basics with textured sweaters and jackets, as well as with flat weaves.

For a complex and sophisticated look, combine beige grey with two other colors, such as terra cotta (figure 22) and deep purple (figure 23), with accents of black. Through careful planning, you can make a versatile and highly personal wardrobe statement without making a major investment.

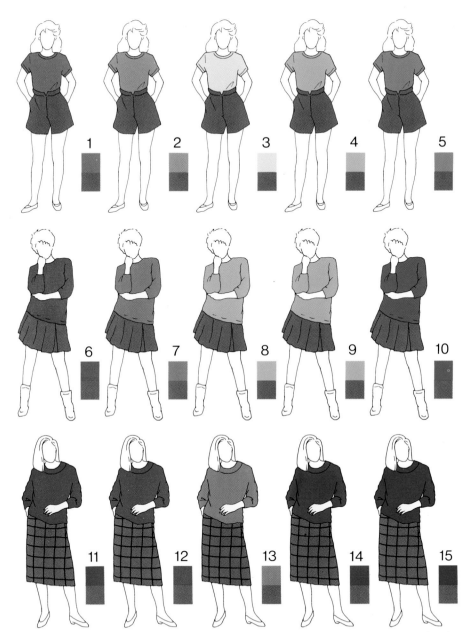

Smoke Brown

Like beige grey, smoke brown is a basic color that mixes easily with a wide range of less versatile colors and that can be worn in summer cottons or winter wools. Smoke brown works well with bright colors (figures 1-15) and offers a refreshing change from black or white for spring and summer dressing.

The brightness of yellow, green, and red overwhelms softer neutrals, but this brown can hold its own when balanced with these brilliant colors.

Mixed with more subdued tones (figures 16-30), smoke brown appears less intense and more tonal than it really is. In figures 16-20, subtle pottery colors mix with brown in a soft, harmonious,

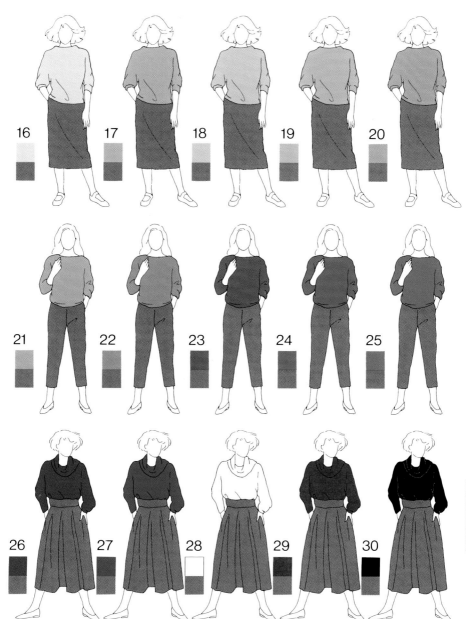

and sophisticated way; although these colors might be difficult to track down, the uniqueness of the combinations will compensate for the effort.

Olive, camel, wine, and blue grey (figures 21-27) are the traditional colors to combine with smoke brown. These mixtures are easy choices for both school and work. Metallic jewelry or accessories can add an elegant finish.

Probably the least interesting colors to pair with smoke brown are off-white, grey, and black (figures 28-30). All three are perfectly wearable mates for this earthy brown, but the other choices on these pages are much more interesting and unusual—take advantage of smoke brown's many unpredictable offerings.

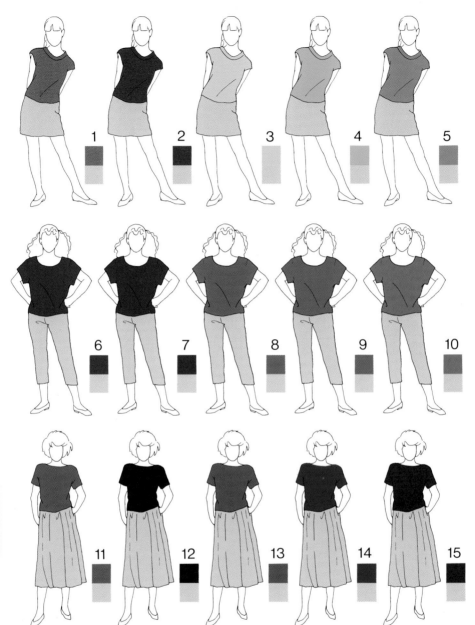

Beige

In French, the word "beige" refers to unbleached wool. This color, however, can be widely used throughout the year in all fabrics. Most people have some beige in their wardrobes already, and these pages show how to use the color in new ways.

Although combinations using pastels (pink, peach, soft aqua) are not shown here, such combinations can work nicely for summer or winter, depending on the fabric.

Beige is difficult to use with the brights in figures 1-10. The dark bright combinations in figures 6-10 work better, but the rich colors in figures 11-18 work best of all. These earth colors are en-

16

17

18

19

20

21

22

23

24

25

26

27

28

29

30

hanced by the neutrality of beige, and the contrasting color—the grape in figure 15 or the mahogany in figure 17—comes alive in the combination. These colors, in either flat or textural weaves, coordinate perfectly for fall.

Beige and the darker tones of blue, grey, brown, and green are comfortable and expected combinations for fall

dressing. The accents of black in figures 21-25 add interest to these neutral combinations, which are particularly appropriate for professional dress.

Beige and black (figure 30) can be impressively chic, especially with the addition of silver or gold jewelry or accessories.

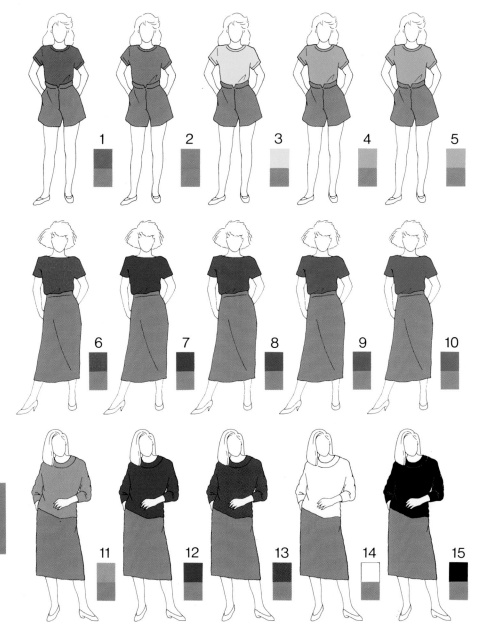

Khaki

Traditionally used as a color for military uniforms or rugged wear, khaki can add an interesting color note to more conventional wardrobes.

Khaki combines with a wide range of colors. Khaki and magenta (figure 1), oxblood (figure 7), and bright navy (figure 12) are all original combinations that work well together.

In summer poplins, khaki worn in shorts, pants, a skirt, or a jacket projects a casual look that is lifted by the dash of color appearing in a solid blouse or sweater or in a bold print.

Because khaki's yellow tone is difficult for most complexions to handle, keep this color away from the face.

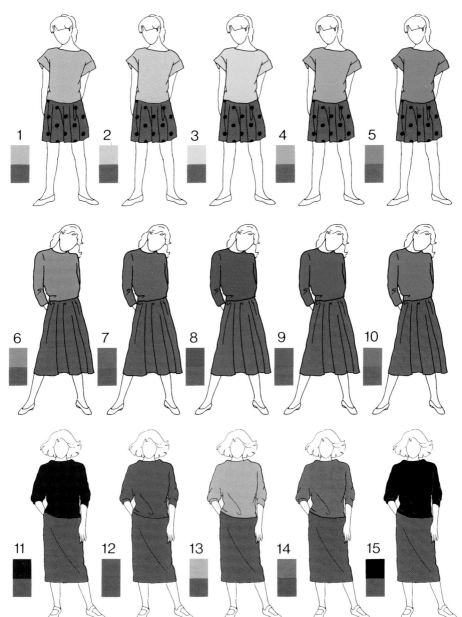

Chestnut

The depth and intensity of this luxurious brown allow it to mix unhesitatingly with red (figure 7) and royal blue (figure 9). Avoid chestnut with lime (figure 3) or turquoise green (figure 4); all other combinations shown are acceptable, intriguing mixes.

The bright/chestnut combinations (figures 5-10) are especially appealing and unusual, but keep the deep brown on the bottom as pants or a skirt.

Chestnut loses its punch when mixed with other browns, grey, or black (figures 11-15). While the combinations are conventionally acceptable, they do not take advantage of the richness of this elegant color.

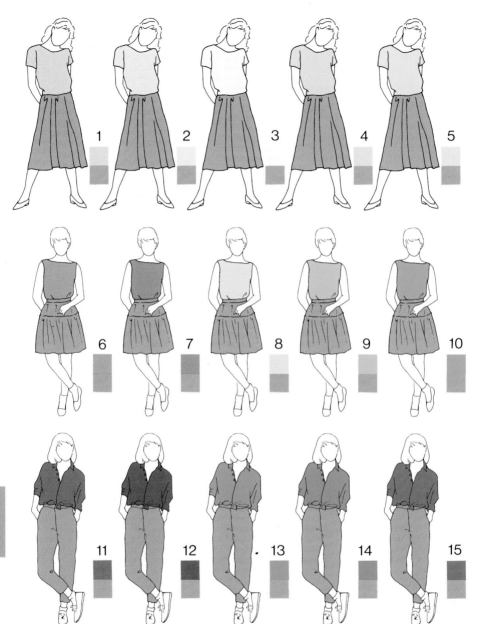

Olive Sand

Unlike the warmer beiges, olive sand has a light green cast that limits the colors it can be coordinated with. This beige effectively mixes with soft earth tones and neutrals, but its delicacy is quickly obliterated by strong colors—even the relatively conservative dark shades in figures 41-45.

Olive sand with any of the soft pastels (figures 1-5) is not an ideal coordination, but consider these mixes for rough-weave summer linens.

The bright colors shown in figures 6-20 overwhelm the beige tone and make it appear flat and greyish.

Olive sand is more suitably matched with the dark jewel tones in figures 21-30

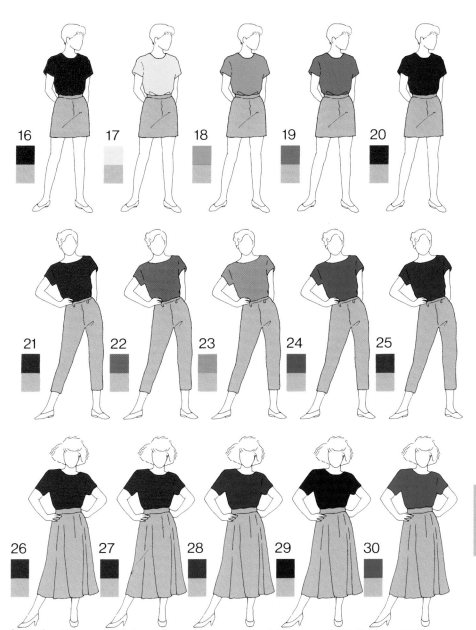

but is best shown with the soft neutrals in figures 31-40, where the coordinating color is not strong enough to overpower the softness of the olive sand.

Olive sand comes into its own when mixed with brown and umber tones (figures 46-50). The black accent strengthens the combinations.

In mixing olive sand with darker and flatter neutrals (figures 51-60), you might expect dull and tedious combinations, but these coordinations are visually appealing and sophisticated. When such a limited color palette is used, tonal relationships become the most important issue.

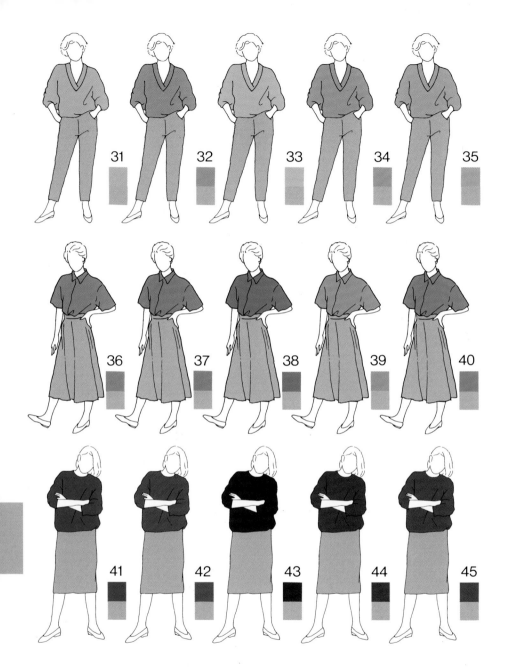

31   32   33   34   35

36   37   38   39   40

41   42   43   44   45

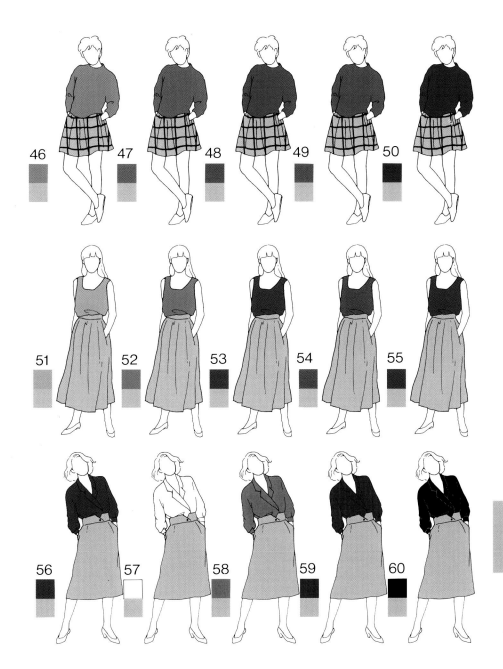

Olive Brown

Olive brown, though it must be used with care and, generally speaking, be kept away from the face, is an immensely popular color that can be found in most summer and winter wardrobes.

For summer, mix olive brown with brights and jewel colors (figures 1-15). The resulting combinations intensify the vivid colors, and the olive becomes a warm and harmonious neutral.

The olive takes on an entirely different personality when combined with soft neutrals (figures 16-20). Here, olive becomes the dominant color, encouraging both warmth and softness in the delicate neutral tones.

Stronger earth tones (figures 21-28)

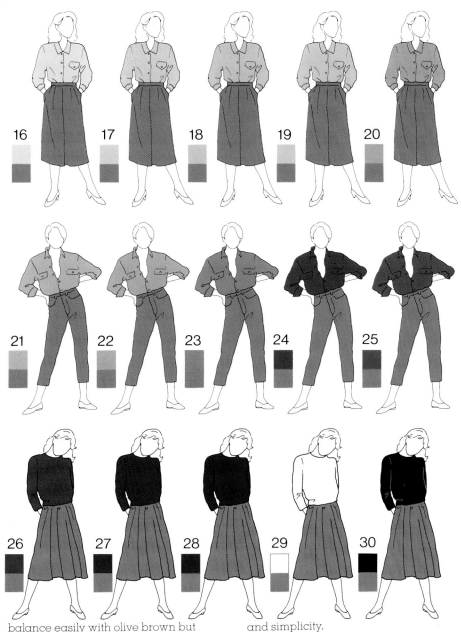

balance easily with olive brown but work best when worn on the top as a sweater, a jacket, or a blouse. These colors would also be compatible in either a plaid or a tweed for fall dressing.

Olive brown combines with off-white (figure 29) or black (figure 30) to create classic mixes that can work any time of year with unfailing success and simplicity.

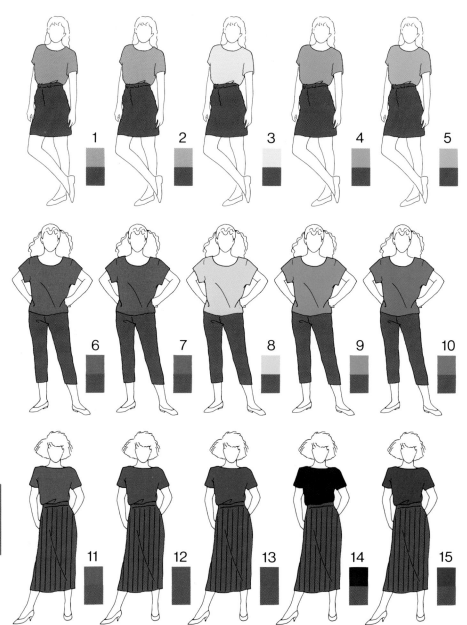

Dark Olive Drab

Dark olive drab is a deeper and more neutral tone than olive green and is probably best known as the uniform color for the U.S. Army. Aside from this institutional use, dark olive drab is also a popular fashion color that can be combined with a broad spectrum of other colors with great effect.

Keep dark olive drab on the bottom as pants or a skirt. Add a brightly colored top from the range of high-colored pastels in figures 1-5, brights in figures 6-10, or jewel brights in figures 11-15. The jewel/dark olive combinations are especially striking and often appear in luxurious woolens in the fall designer collections.

The olive character of the color

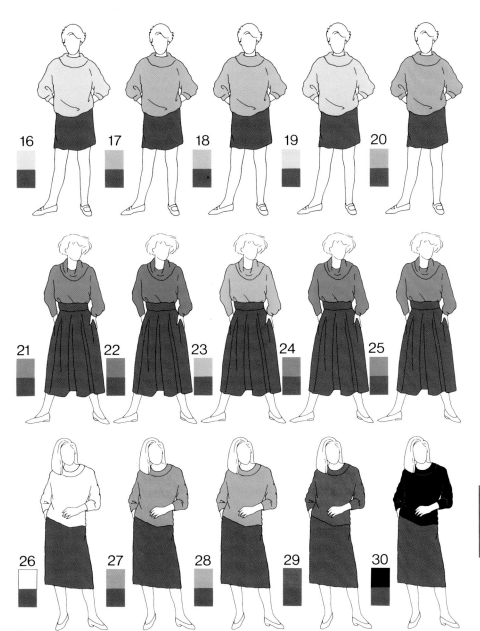

becomes apparent when it is mixed with soft, earth-toned pastels (figures 16-20). These visually appealing combinations can be worn easily by people with a variety of complexions and colorings.

The cinnamon, ocher, and teal blue combinations (figures 21-25) are natural choices for fall wardrobes. These colors would mix beautifully in a wool challis

print worn with a simple, cowled sweater in a soft wool blend.

When combined with neutrals and monotones (figures 26-30), dark olive drab appears harsh. Clearly, this color has an affinity for brightness and tonal depth. Wear this olive in ways that it can take advantage of such qualities.

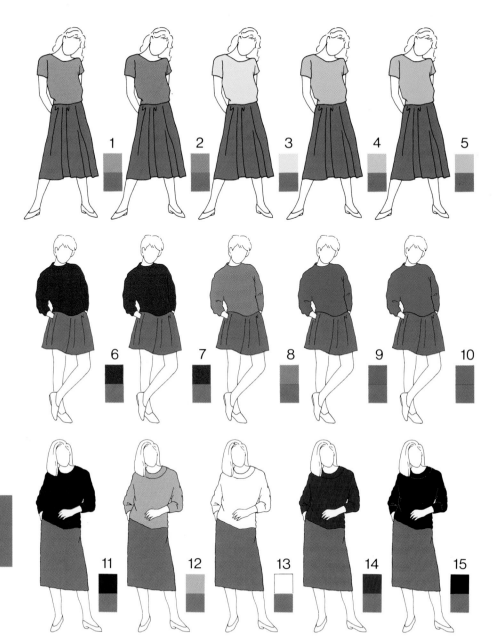

Celadon Grey

Sophisticated celadon grey is unique because of its greenish cast and versatile because it works with other greys.

Brilliant brights (figures 1-10) overwhelm celadon—the brights become brighter, and the delicate grey-green fades into unimportance.

Celadon works much better when combined with earth tones (beige in figure 11 or charcoal grey in figure 14).

Celadon with black (figure 15) can be striking, especially if gold jewelry is added as an accent to bring warmth to the combination.

With off-white (figure 13), celadon can be elegant in fine fabrics such as silk and fine wool.

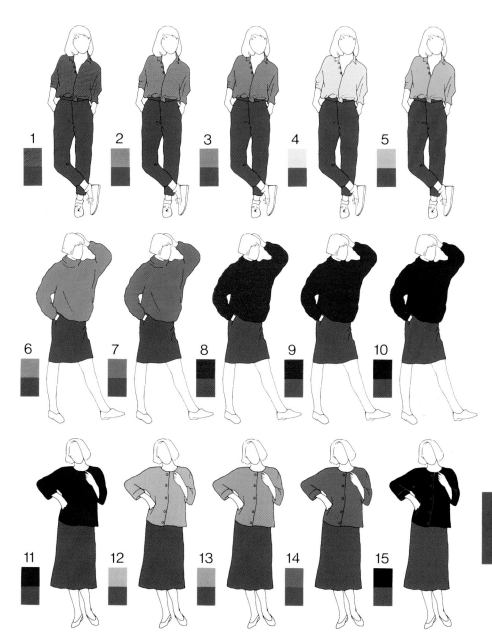

Slate Green

Slate green acts the opposite of celadon grey. The hardness of this color requires the intense brightness of red, yellow, and turquoise to balance slate green's strong personality.

Figures 1-10 offer some interesting ideas for autumn dressing. The brown, umber, and orange tones in figures 2, 3,

6, and 7 appear as new, exciting colors when mixed with slate green.

The slate green/dark neutral mixes in figures 11-15 are less interesting conceptually but are completely acceptable in a conventional sense. Like chestnut, however, slate green works best when challenged and enhanced with vivid color.

93

Lead Grey

This cool, bluish grey is unusual in
coordinated sportswear. The primary
importance of lead grey is apparent
in men's wear, where this color is com-
monly used in three-piece suits as a
solid or a pin-striped weave.

Paired with strong, bright colors
(figures 1-10), lead grey stands up well,

even to the vivid tones of rose carmine
(figure 7) and parrot green (figure 9).
Matched with bright pastels (figures
1-5), lead grey creates softer and more
harmonious combinations than black
or navy does.

Lead grey and black (figure 15)
creates an elegant alternative that can
be lightened with white or pastel accents.

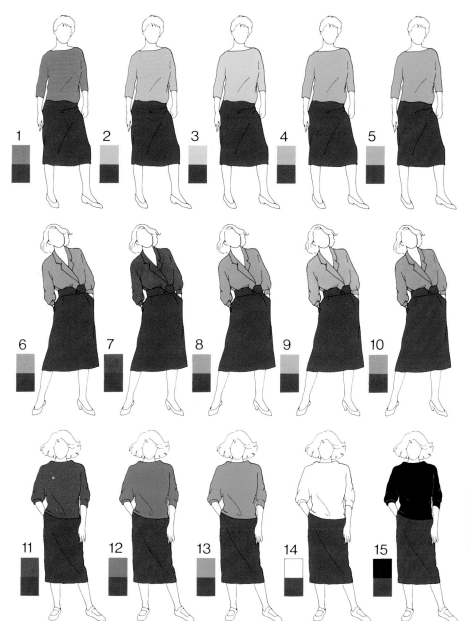

Damson

Damson, an intriguing and rare color that combines nicely with other earth tones, does not mix well with soft brights (figures 1-5) or brighter brights (figures 11-13). When kept to combinations within its own tonal family (figures 6-10), however, damson can offer a subtle and appealing alternative to a flatter and more traditional brown or grey tone.

Off-white and black (figures 14 and 15) also mix nicely with damson. This color has a depth and distinctiveness that should be pursued and expanded—consider adding dramatic jewelry or accessories in warm metallic tones.

Cardigan Sweater, Pleated Skirt, Tie

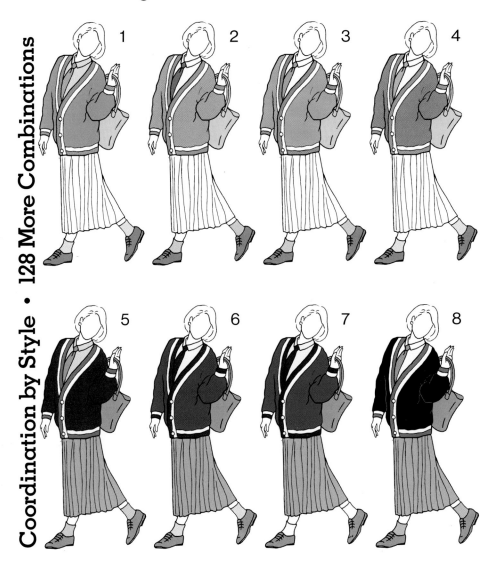

In these combinations, you can see how the feeling of the outfit changes as you move around the colors. The styling is easy—an overscaled preppie look. Note how this classic combination can reflect any season, depending on the color combination and, of course, the fabric.

The color combinations in figures 1-4 suggest spring dressing because of the white skirt and bright colors, even though the color mixing is unusual. Navy with white is classic for this look, but consider grey, pink, and green for a refreshing and charming change.

Figures 5-8 show a grey, pleated skirt paired in a more traditional way with red, navy, green, and brown cardigans. The red/grey combination

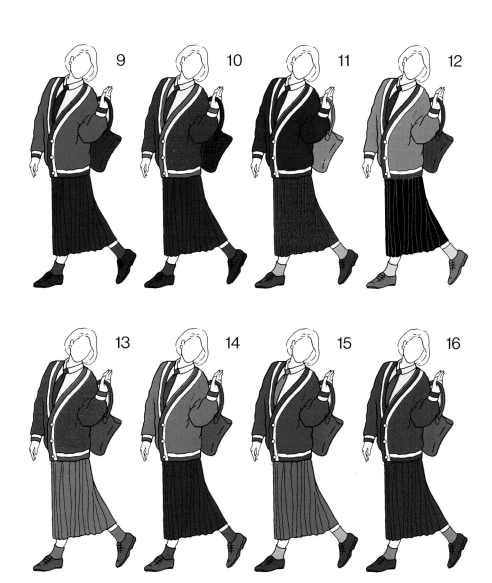

has lots of zip when accented with a pink shirt and green tie. The other combinations are oriented more to men's wear, using conventional color combinations and letting the tie act as the accent.

Similar color feelings are present in combinations 9-16. The prevailing image is men's wear, and the combina-

tions represent traditional fall colors. In these coordinates, note that the stockings can be an inventive accent to individualize your look. Study these combinations. If you haven't considered mixing red with brown (figure 13), try it. It's a warm, fall combination that wears well on both light and dark complexions.

Pullover Sweater, Big Shirt, Pegged Pants

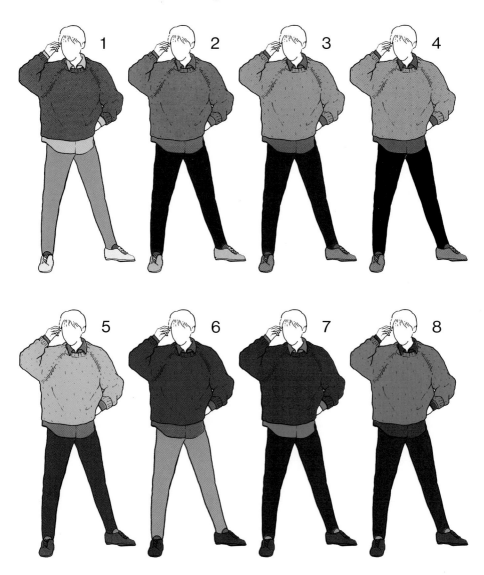

This wonderfully casual look can be worn by any age and still look young. Because the volume of the material is on the top, the hips and legs look slim. With this sporty look, the colors can contrast brightly—actually, the more unusual, the better. Use the shirt as the accent as in figure 7, where the green complements the red and adds the zip that

makes this outfit special. In figure 4, the tone-on-tone in the shirt and sweater creates a layered effect suggesting more of a texture than a color statement.

Be daring. A few years ago, figures 3 and 5 would have been considered garish and in the worst taste. Now, of course, they are the last word.

V-Neck Sweater, Soft Gathered Skirt, Patterned Shirt

This slight exaggeration of a classic silhouette is feminine and soft. The basically conservative look particularly suits fall dressing but can be easily translated into linens and soft colors for spring wardrobes.

In figures 1-8, the skirt color stays on the conservative side; the color interest emerges in the relationship between the shirt and the sweater. Although the sweater colors are fairly basic, the combination can become more fashionable when an unusual color is for the shirt (figure 6) or more conservative when a tonally compatible shirt is used (figure 4). Again, note how both shoes and anklets can be used as accessory color accents.

Cardigan Sweater, Sweater, Skirt

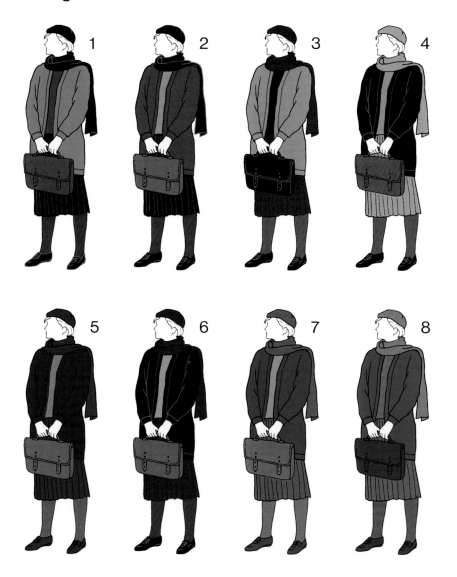

For this obviously wooly winter look, accessories like the beret and muffler add the final touch.

Figures 1-16 show interesting and unusual color combinations for winter. Consider the different ways to combine red, grey, and black (figures 1-2), or for an unexpected accent to black, add peach (figure 4).

The jewel tones in figures 5-8 combine well with and brighten winter wools, and these outfits are tonally mixed to achieve a rich, refined look.

Browns are attractively combined with winter white (figure 11), coral (figure 10), and pink and grey (figure 9). While the effect would be too flat in cotton, the warmth of the woolen texture

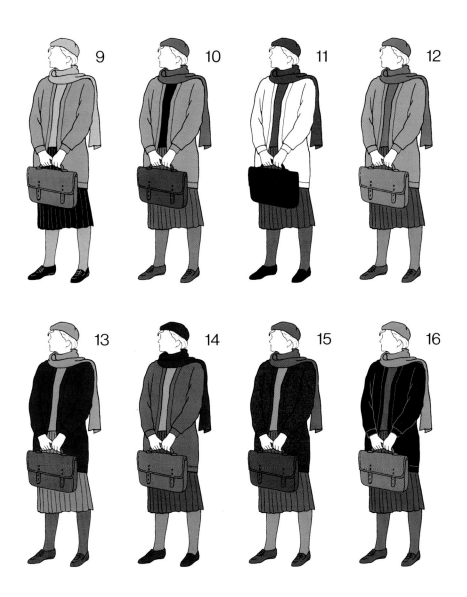

compensates for the coolness of the
colors.

    Figures 13-16 present conventional
color combinations—browns with blues
(figures 14-15) and black (figure 16). In
figure 13, notice how the coral adds a
spark of color.

Jacket, Sweater or T-Shirt

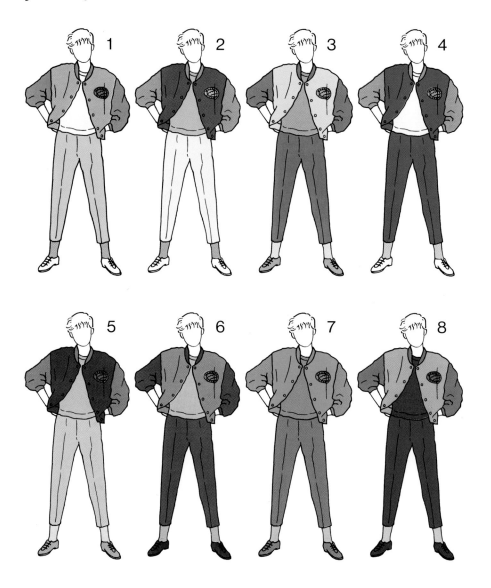

Even if this decidedly young look isn't you, study the color combinations for some fresh and unusual ideas. The medium pastels mixed with greys and beiges in figures 1-4 suggest a sweet, yet chic, junior look.

In figures 5-8, peach, pink, turquoise, and ocher are appealingly combined with grey and brown neutrals.

These unique color combinations are rather unlikely, but they work well in a casual, sporty way when you use color-blocking.

The combinations in figures 9-16 are traditional, but each outfit has an almost patchwork effect because so many different colors are blocked in one coordination. The black plaid worked

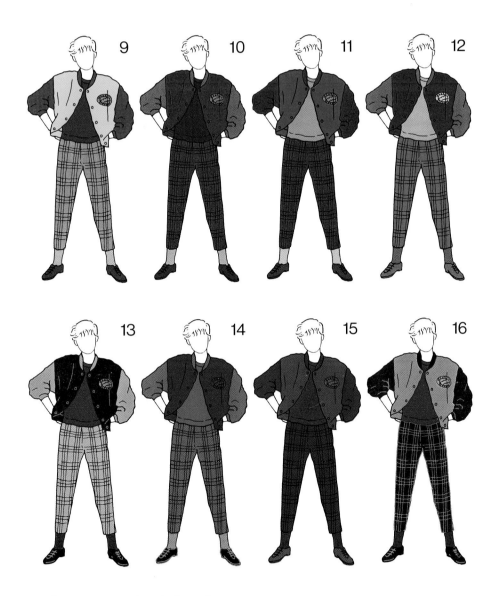

into the pants gives the whole outfit a
young, boyish look. The technique of
color-blocking works in most of the 16
combinations because the color tones
are similar even if the colors themselves
are very different. Color-blocking does
not work in figure 9, where a poison
green color is used, creating a strong,
almost shocking visual image.

Jacket, Sailor Top, Straight Skirt

Figures 1-16 show how different visual effects can be achieved through layering. Whether color-layering is used tonally to create a textural effect or contrasting blocks of color are used to achieve a printlike feeling, layering can effectively combine your existing wardrobe in a new way.

Bright pastels combined tonally (figures 1-4) create a spring look that could also work in winter woolens.

The aggressive, contrasting combinations in figures 5-8 represent winter cotton and sweatshirt mixes for the young and daring—the poison green with orange in figure 5 is only for the *very* young and *very* daring. All of these figures, however, make a strong fashion

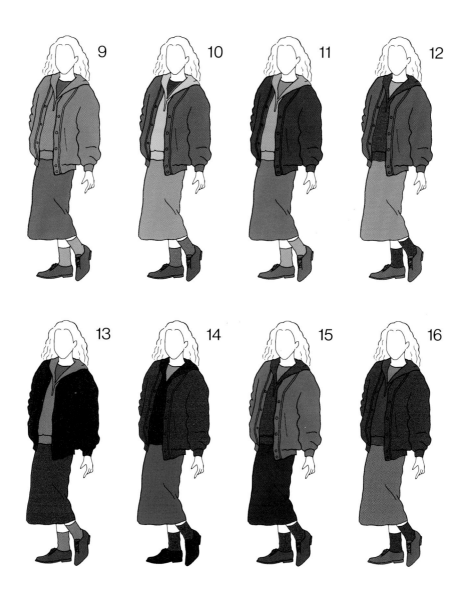

statement in which the combination is more than its colored parts.

The bright colors used in jackets in figures 5-8 are used as accents in the sailor tops in figures 9-12. This coordination is easier to wear, and the splash of color adds just enough interest to make the earth colors in the jackets and skirts look chic rather than drab—use this technique in winter dressing, which can become tedious otherwise.

In figures 13-16, jewel tones are combined with bright red and touches of orange for a bright winter, layered look. Brown is also introduced to keep the combinations autumnal in feeling and to ensure that the jewel tones don't become too bright or harsh.

Blazer, Sweater, Skirt, Blouse

While the blazer, sweater, and skirt combination has become almost a uniform for the working woman, these two pages show how an inventive use of color can make an often mundane combination into something interesting and unusual without being inappropriate for the professional woman.

In figures 1-2, pink is used as an accent with navy and grey and with red and grey. The latter color mix used to be considered a clashing combination but is now quite acceptable.

Navy blue and grey are traditional blazer combination colors, but the dusty pastels combined with blue grey, cream, and light grey (figures 5-8) create a surprisingly nice image that

would be wonderful in a linen fabric for summer and spring dressing.

The conventional browns in figures 9-12 are easily mixed for a clean, professional look. If these combinations appear a bit boring, add more color (figures 13-16) to make them interesting yet still not too bright for the office.

Jacket, Shirt, Pants

The oversized blazer has enjoyed enormous popularity over the past seasons. Besides being an important piece functionally, it can be a fashion accessory useful in a variety of fabrics and colors. In figures 1-5, the jacket in neutrals is paired with pants and a bright shirt for an easy and modern image—a look for everyone.

In figures 6-10, the same neutral jacket is combined with dark pants. With a bright shirt for a visual snap, this look is still easy for anyone to understand.

Fashion takes over in figures 9-12, where the jacket is shown in combination with contrasting colors that create an appealing and forward fashion

image.

The color-blocking is still bright in figures 13-16, but a neutral shirt and dark pants make the look easier to wear.

Jacket, Blouse, Skirt

The styles and colors shown on these two pages represent what has become known as career dressing. This section should be a favorite for those women who feel boxed in by the rather strict dress codes of the office environment. This look is clean and conservative in styling, but the use of fabrics that have softness or movement and that use color as an accessory creates a business-like but feminine look embraced by a majority of professional women. Color coordination is an important and sensitive issue here. If the colors are too monochrome and dark, the outfit will become heavy and ominous looking because the styling is so simple—almost uniformlike. On the other hand, while

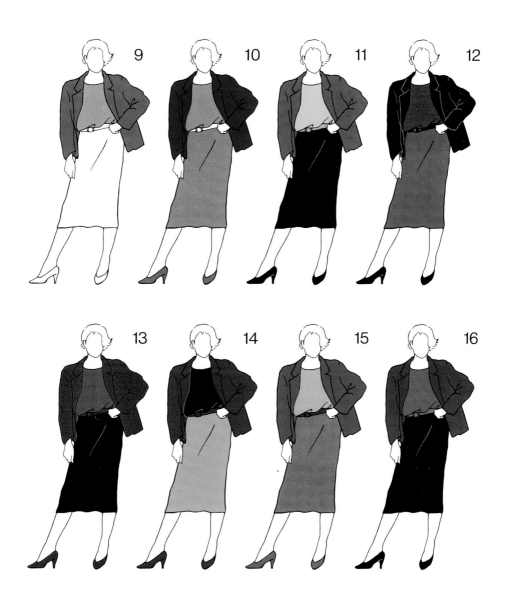

most professional women want *some* color, they abhor colors that are too strong or color contrasts that might make them stand out.

Figures 1-6 offer a variety of options —all tasteful but showing some individuality and personal fashion expression. Notice how important the shoes become as a fashion accessory. Jewelry, particularly earrings and eyeglasses, can also be important components in this look.

Study the figures carefully and note how much variety can be achieved by rethinking traditional color combinations.

Color Gallery of Accessories

1
2
3
4
5
6
7
8
9
10
11
12
13
14
15
16
17
18
19
20

The accent colors you wear in accessories—shoes, stockings, jewelry, belts—are as important as the basic color of your dress or suit. Accent colors are control colors: they can be as dark as the number 12 in figure 38 or as bright as the example in figure 14; the important thing to remember is that

21   22   23   24

25   26   27   28

29   30   31   32

33   34   35   36

37   38   39   40

accents emphasize your original
concept and complete the outfit.
　　Study the way small amounts of
color are used to alter and accentuate

the personality of the garments in the
next eleven pages. Consider the
combinations that work for you and why.
Then focus on your own wardrobe and

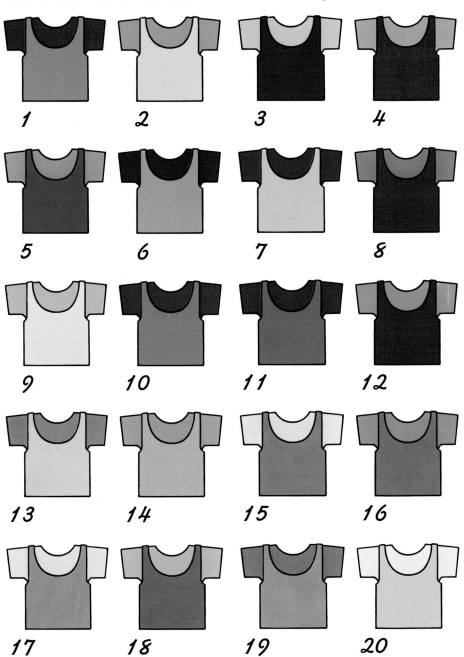

1　　2　　3　　4

5　　6　　7　　8

9　　10　　11　　12

13　　14　　15　　16

17　　18　　19　　20

use accent colors to assert your individuality and project your own image.

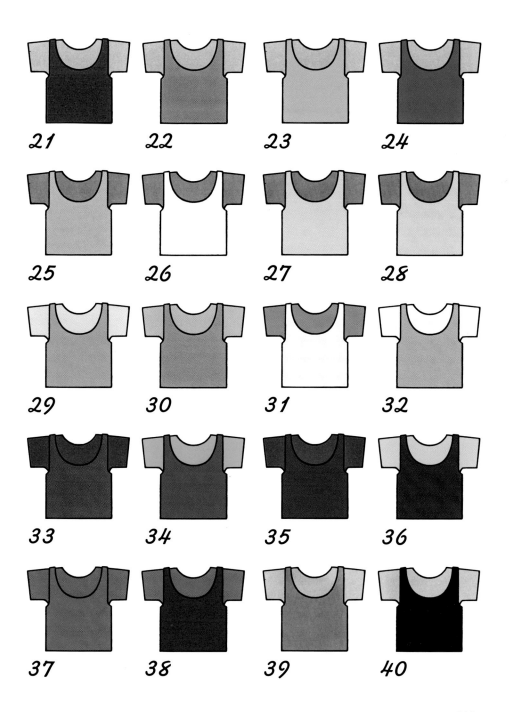

21 22 23 24

25 26 27 28

29 30 31 32

33 34 35 36

37 38 39 40

1   2   3   4

5   6   7   8

9   10   11   12

13   14   15   16

17   18   19   20

21 22 23 24

25 26 27 28

29 30 31 32

33 34 35 36

37 38 39 40

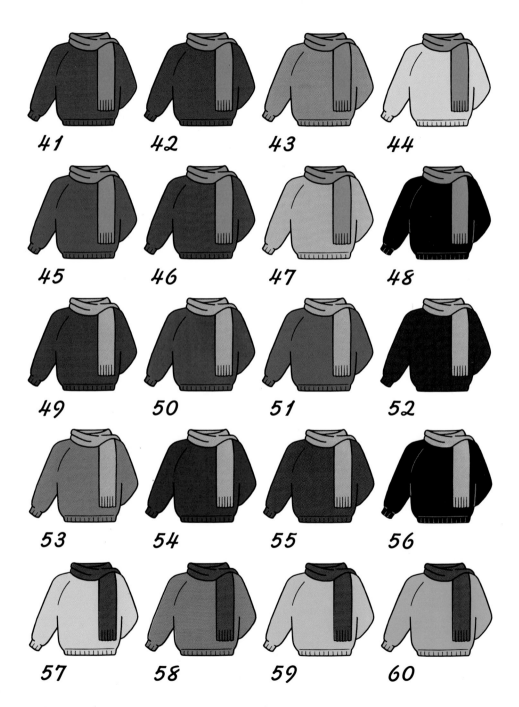

41 42 43 44

45 46 47 48

49 50 51 52

53 54 55 56

57 58 59 60

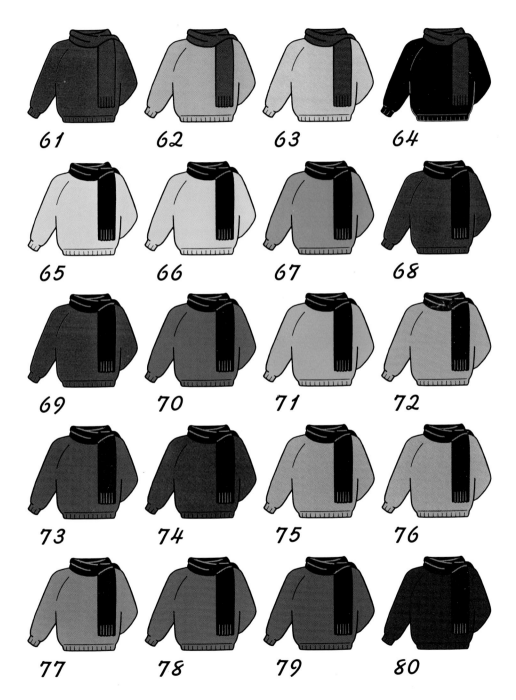

61   62   63   64

65   66   67   68

69   70   71   72

73   74   75   76

77   78   79   80

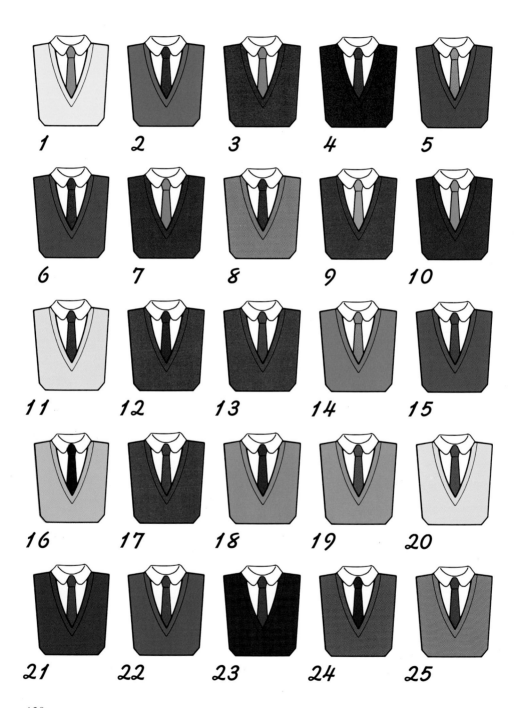

1   2   3   4   5

6   7   8   9   10

11   12   13   14   15

16   17   18   19   20

21   22   23   24   25

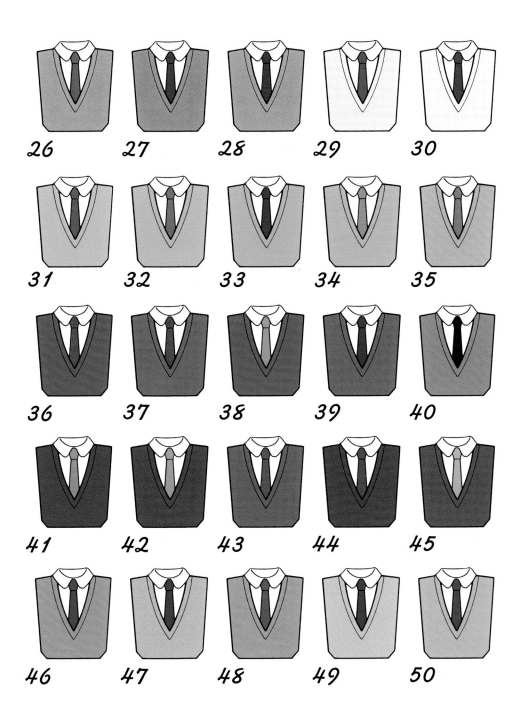

26   27   28   29   30

31   32   33   34   35

36   37   38   39   40

41   42   43   44   45

46   47   48   49   50

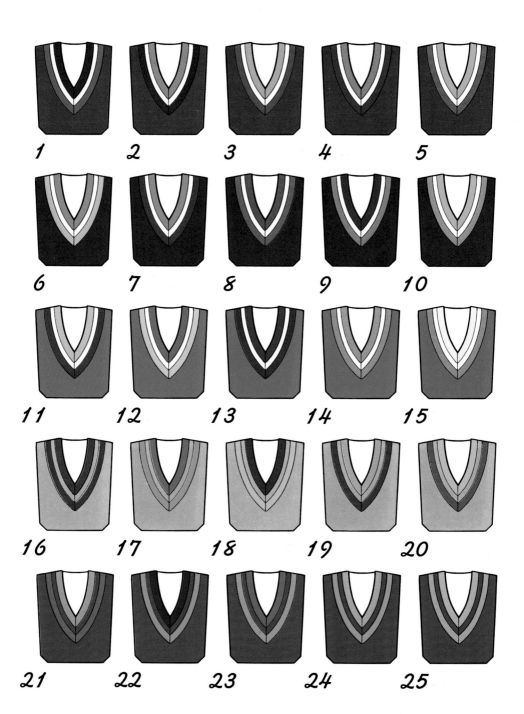

150 Colors and Their Names

* Starred colors are shown in combination with other colors in figures 4 through 95.

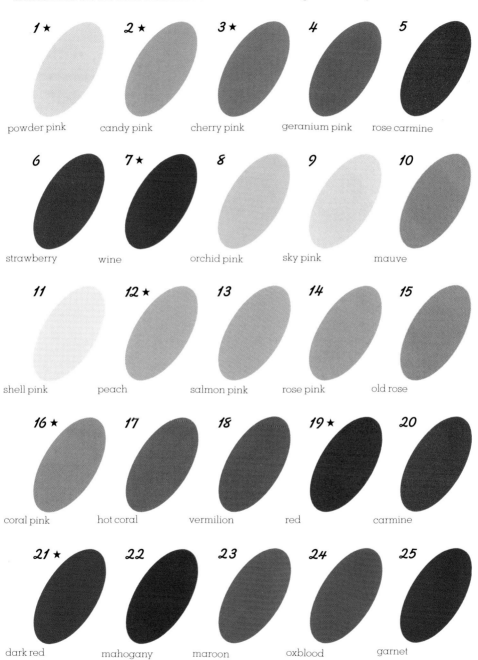

1 ★ powder pink

2 ★ candy pink

3 ★ cherry pink

4 geranium pink

5 rose carmine

6 strawberry

7 ★ wine

8 orchid pink

9 sky pink

10 mauve

11 shell pink

12 ★ peach

13 salmon pink

14 rose pink

15 old rose

16 ★ coral pink

17 hot coral

18 vermilion

19 ★ red

20 carmine

21 ★ dark red

22 mahogany

23 maroon

24 oxblood

25 garnet

26 apricot

27 tangerine orange

28 marigold

29 ★ orange

30 burnt orange

31 butterscotch

32 ★ brown gold

33 yellow ocher

34 camel

35 cinnamon

36 cork

37 dijon

38 ivory

39 ★ beige

40 tan

41 burnt sienna

42 terra cotta

43 umber

44 tobacco brown

45 cocoa

46 deep maroon

47 ★ chestnut

48 ★ smoke brown

49 chocolate

50 ★ sepia

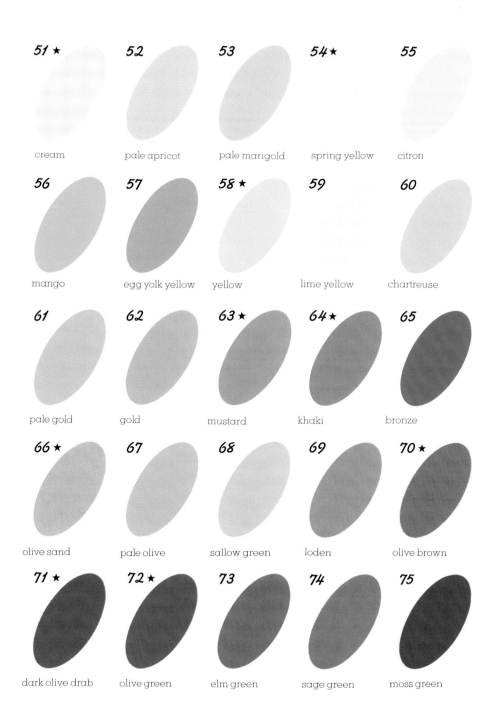

51 ★ cream

52 pale apricot

53 pale marigold

54 ★ spring yellow

55 citron

56 mango

57 egg yolk yellow

58 ★ yellow

59 lime yellow

60 chartreuse

61 pale gold

62 gold

63 ★ mustard

64 ★ khaki

65 bronze

66 ★ olive sand

67 pale olive

68 sallow green

69 loden

70 ★ olive brown

71 ★ dark olive drab

72 ★ olive green

73 elm green

74 sage green

75 moss green

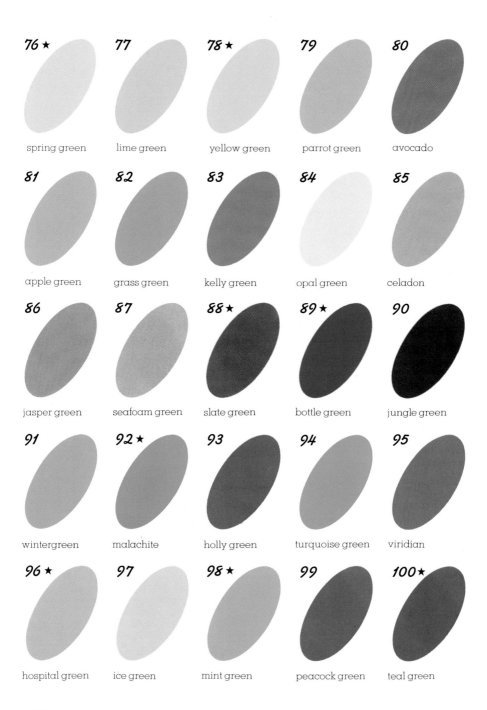

76 ★ spring green

77 lime green

78 ★ yellow green

79 parrot green

80 avocado

81 apple green

82 grass green

83 kelly green

84 opal green

85 celadon

86 jasper green

87 seafoam green

88 ★ slate green

89 ★ bottle green

90 jungle green

91 wintergreen

92 ★ malachite

93 holly green

94 turquoise green

95 viridian

96 ★ hospital green

97 ice green

98 ★ mint green

99 peacock green

100 ★ teal green

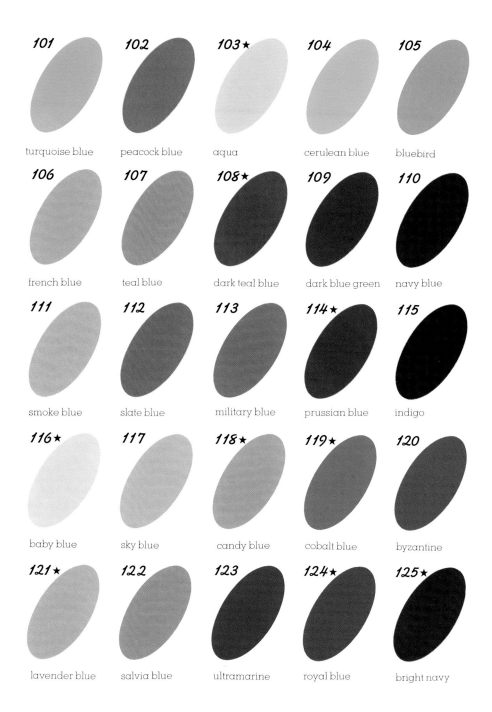

101 turquoise blue	**102** peacock blue	**103 ★** aqua	**104** cerulean blue	**105** bluebird
106 french blue	**107** teal blue	**108 ★** dark teal blue	**109** dark blue green	**110** navy blue
111 smoke blue	**112** slate blue	**113** military blue	**114 ★** prussian blue	**115** indigo
116 ★ baby blue	**117** sky blue	**118 ★** candy blue	**119 ★** cobalt blue	**120** byzantine
121 ★ lavender blue	**122** salvia blue	**123** ultramarine	**124 ★** royal blue	**125 ★** bright navy

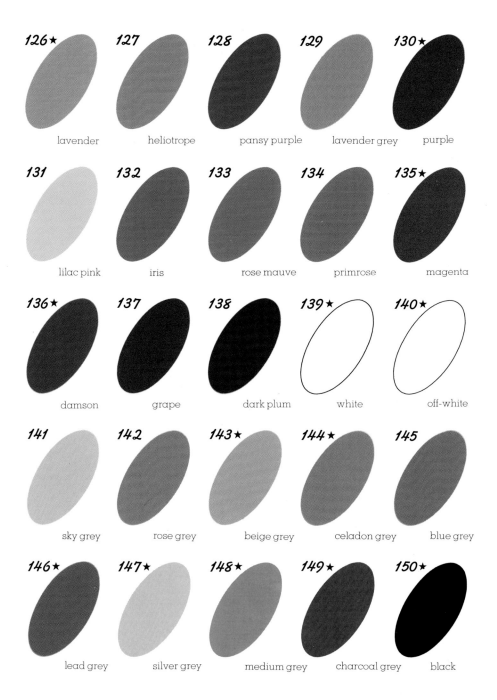

126 ★	*127*	*128*	*129*	*130* ★
lavender	heliotrope	pansy purple	lavender grey	purple
131	*132*	*133*	*134*	*135* ★
lilac pink	iris	rose mauve	primrose	magenta
136 ★	*137*	*138*	*139* ★	*140* ★
damson	grape	dark plum	white	off-white
141	*142*	*143* ★	*144* ★	*145*
sky grey	rose grey	beige grey	celadon grey	blue grey
146 ★	*147* ★	*148* ★	*149* ★	*150* ★
lead grey	silver grey	medium grey	charcoal grey	black

Appendix

Dictionary of Commonly Used Fashion Terms

Accordion pleats: Fold of ¼″ to ¾″ in width in cloth.

Achromatic color: Black or white; that which has no color; a non-color.

Advancing color: A color that appears to come forward in a pattern; red, yellow, and yellow-green are examples.

African print: A dynamic and colorful print, taken from traditional African dress and textiles.

All-weather coat: A coat that can be worn in fine or inclement weather.

Alpaca: Cloth woven from the brown or black wool of the alpaca, a South American mammal.

American style: In contrast to European or Japanese styles; typically, this style is sporty, preppie, casual, and easygoing.

Animal print: A cloth pattern representing the skin of an exotic animal, such as a zebra or a leopard.

Antique: In the style of a former period; describing accessories that evoke a nostalgia for the past.

Apparel industry: The enterprise of manufacturing textiles and clothing.

Arabesque: A style of cloth featuring oriental patterns with abstract, geometric, or swirling motif.

Argyle: A Scottish pattern of diamond shapes in three basic colors; most often used in socks and sweaters.

Army look: The shape or color (usually army green or dark olive drab) of a military uniform.

Art deco: The decorative and fine arts movement that began in France and England in the early twenties. Characterized by stylish, geometric patterns; typical colors used are purple, yellow, green, gold, silver, and black.

Art nouveau: Decorative and fine art born in France, Germany, Belgium, and Austria in the late 19th century. Linear and curvilinear designs applied to crafts and buildings, including the Paris subway stations.

Asymmetry: Without symmetry; unbalanced; used to create movement by breaking the symmetry.

Backless: Exposing the back; used to describe swimsuit and dress design.

Baggies: Pants that are fitted at the waist and hips but full in the legs; adapted from European styles of the seventies.

Bandanna: A cotton scarf, often with paisley or calico patterns; derived from the term for a particular method of dyeing cloth in India.

Basic color: In determining color schemes, one of the major colors to choose from—often black, beige, white, or grey.

Bell bottom: A flared pant leg; popular in the early seventies.

Blazer: A long-sleeved sports jacket with lapels; sometimes with a crest on the breast pocket.

Bleached: Whitened; describing clothes from which all color has been removed; for example, bleached-out jeans.

Blousing: Gathering a blouse or dress in at the waist.

Blouson: A women's jacket or shirt that blouses and is drawn in at the waist or slightly below the waist.

Border print: A design that runs along a hem or cuff.

Bottom: Clothing worn below the waist, such as pants or a skirt.

Bow tie: A small necktie with two loops worn at the neck for both casual and formal wear.

Bulky: Large, loose-fitting; characteristic of sweaters of coats made of thick yarn.

Burberry: A high-quality, traditional raincoat manufactured by Burberry; descriptive of coats in that style.

Button-down: Fastened down with buttons; a shirt with the collar fastened in this way; an indispensable article for the Ivy League look.

Camouflage: A design incorporating the army's brown-green camouflage print; the army look.

Career dressing: A dress code for the professional woman. Usually a conservative look styled to fit into what was originally "a man's world." The basic look includes a tailored blazer, a straight skirt, and a detailed blouse.

Casual wear: Informal, everyday clothing, typical of the American lifestyle.

Chambray: A smooth cotton fabric, made by weaving colored thread vertically across horizontal thread of another color.

Chanel suit: A woman's suit designed by the French designer Gabrielle "Coco" Chanel; simple skirt and short, collarless jacket.

Check-on-check: Having various layered check patterns and colors.

Chic: Sophisticated or stylish.

Chinois: Chinese style.

Cine mode: A style of fashion that originated in the movies—the Annie Hall look or the Gatsby look.

Circle skirt: A skirt—made by cutting cloth into a circle, with the waist at the center—so full that it makes wave-like motion.

City wear: Street dress that has a sophisticated fashion image.

Classic: Traditional, timeless. Describing styles that have been popular for a long time. Fashion is an ongoing cycle of new trendy and classic styles.

Classic prints: Patterns, such as paisley and foulard, which are not affected by fashion trends.

Cobalt colors: Hot colors made popular in the sixties. High-intensity blue, red, yellow, and green were the major colors making up this group.

Collection: A preseason showing of a designer's line; usually held twice a year for spring/summer and fall/winter fashions.

Color-blocking: Placing equivalent amounts of color side by side within a single garment to make a visual color statement. In fine art, Mondrian was the greatest of all color-blockers.

Color coordination: The planning of an outfit by considering the relationships of the colors to be worn.

Complex harmony: Harmonious color schemes created with colors that are usually incompatible; a combination that makes red/yellow colors dark and blue/green colors bright—turquoise and dark brown, for example.

Conservative: Traditional; staying away from fashion trends and keeping to traditional styles.

Contemporary: Current; having the look of today; the now look.

Continental: Characteristic of European men's styles, featuring wide shoulders, fitted waists, and short lengths.

Cool colors: Colors with a blue undertone and suggesting serenity. Cool colors include blue, green, and purple.

Corduroy: Derived from the French term "cor du roi," meaning cloth of the French royalty; like denim, widely used by people of all ages.

Cosmetic color: A color relating to makeup for the face; for example, peach, pink, beige.

Cosmopolitan: Sophisticated, international; describing the behavior or dress of a citizen of the world, rather than a citizen of any one country.

Costume: Stylized and coordinated clothes or dress based on a theme or story.

Costume jewelry: Originally, inexpensive jewelry used in a play; today, accessories.

Country look: An appearance evoked by wearing traditional tweeds or wovens typical of the English country gentleman.

Crêpe process: The procedure involved in shrinking the surface of silk, rayon, and acetate to create an elegant shininess.

Crew neck: The round neck of a sweater or T-shirt.

Culottes: Originally, short pants worn by men in late 17th and early 18th century France; today, a divided skirt for contemporary fashion.

Designer: One who initiates new fabric concepts, either in a sketch or with the actual fabric.

Dolman: Describing a sleeve cut very wide at the shoulders and tapered at the wrists.

Down jacket: A jacket filled with goose or duck down for insulation against the cold.

Drape: The way a fabric falls or hangs on the body.

Duffle coat: A short, hooded coat fastened with wooden buttons and rope loops.

Dungaree: Originally, a coarse cotton cloth (denim) made in India and used to make work clothes; now, denim jeans.

Earth colors: Colors that are found in nature and relate to the brown family—sienna, ocher, brown tones, and dark green. Natural plant dyes are often used to color natural fibers.

Electric color: A brilliant color.

Elegance: Grace and sophistication in clothing.

Emblem: A symbol or badge.

Ensemble: An outfit with a look of unity and coordination; often one material is used for all pieces of the outfit.

Espadrille: A kind of sandal made of hemp and canvas and originally worn by the Basque people. Made popular by surfers in this country; a favorite of young women in the seventies.

Ethnic: Native, traditional.

Exoticism: Interest in ethnic clothing styles or clothes evoking a foreign land; as used in the U.S. and Europe, interest in the designs based on the traditional clothing of people in the Orient, Middle East, and Africa.

Fabric: A material, such as cloth, made from fibers by weaving, knitting, felting, etc.

Fake fur: Artificial fur made from synthetic material.

Fanny wrap: Sash or cloth draped at the hips for an elegant streamlined effect.

Fantastic: Imaginary, romantic, dream-like.

Fashion coordinator: A specialist in the wearing of fashion clothes.

Fashion-forward: At the forefront of a new fashion trend. Also called "advanced fashion." The opposite of classic or basic dressing.

Fashion victims: Unfortunate beings who think only about being first in the latest look, with little thought given to how the fashion looks on them. These fashion groupies usually wear extreme, bizarre fashion.

Fifties: Describing fifties clothing, which emphasized the silhouette; rock-and-roll fashion. Typical colors used were pink, black, grey, and aqua.

Fisherman knit sweater: Thick, multi-patterned sweater copied from sweaters worn by fishermen in northern Europe.

Flannel: A soft cotton weave, usually printed in a striped or checked pattern; for jackets and pants.

Flapper: In the twenties, a woman who was considered daring for wearing different fashions. The bobbed hair style is sometimes called "the flapper."

Flare: Describing bias-cut clothing that creates a sleek, linear image; for example, the flare skirt.

Folkloric: Characteristic of ethnic styles.

Formal: Describing a dress code requiring evening dress for women, tuxedos for men.

Foulard: A lightweight fabric of silk, rayon, etc., usually printed with small figures, such as a fleur-de-lis pattern.

Foundation: An undergarment to smooth the figure; basic facial cosmetics.

Garcon look: A boyish fashion worn by women.

Gingham: A plain weave in checks or stripes.

Glen check: A blue and white suit-check for men or women.

Gradations: Shades of color. Unity is created by related shades or contrasting colors.

Gun club checks: A pattern of double checks—often in white, black, and red-brown—used for jackets.

Haberdashery look: An appearance evoked by combining several tailored men's wear prints and textures in one outfit. The jacket and shirt shapes also suggest a men's wear look.

Hand: The texture and weight of a fabric; more specifically, the quality of the weave.

Haute couture: Literally, "high sewing," referring to the original designs—usually custom-made by Saint Laurent or Ungaro—of the European fashion houses. Very expensive.

Hawaiian shirt: A short-sleeved shirt in bright tropical prints.

High fashion: Haute couture before it becomes current fashion.

High tech: Advanced industrial technology; in fashion, an ultramodern look.

Hip hugger: Pants or a skirt with the waist line resting on the hips; popular in the sixties.

Hippie style: Style of the flower children of the sixties; characterized by long hair on men and women, beards, blue jeans, and psychedelic colors.

Houndstooth: Pointed check pattern woven into fabric for men's and women's fashion.

Ichimatsu check: A pattern in which two squares of color are used alternately in fabric. Derived from the costume of Japanese Kabuki actor Sanogawa Ichimatsu (19th century). Also known as benroku pattern.

Imitation: A fake or copy, usually of furs or jewelry. Cheaper than the real thing, fake accessories and furs have been very popular in recent seasons.

Impact color: Pure color used to create a shocking effect; for example, a bright red fire engine.

Inner wear: General term describing any clothing worn under a coat or jacket.

Iridescent: Having or showing an interplay of rainbow-like colors. A look achieved by weaving together two different kinds of fibers, such as rayon and polyester.

Ivy League: A popular look for men in the fifties that originated on such campuses as Harvard, Princeton, and Yale; a forerunner to the preppie look; a style characterized by button-down collar shirts and pants with a small buckle in the back.

Jeans: Originally, work clothes made of denim. In the sixties, denim jeans became big fashion, and the style spread worldwide.

Jewel tones: Deep hues of red, blue, green, and purple with the richness and intensity of fine gems.

Jump suit: A coverall or one-piece garment with pants; popular as casual fashion in the seventies and eighties.

Jungle print: A pattern depicting African plants, animals, or other elements of African culture.

Junk jewelry: Imitation jewelry; fun accessories.

Khaki: A color name that means "earth" in Hindi and indicates a dark or greenish yellow; often, a military or safari color.

Kimono sleeve: A sleeve with no distinct separation from the jacket or robe; used to describe the sleeve shape of the Japanese kimono.

Knickers: Knickerbockers. In the late 19th century, men's short pants designed for bicycle riding; these often enjoy a fashion revival. In England, knickers are underpants.

Knockoffs: Inexpensive copies of high-priced designer fashion.

Lacy knit: A weave constructed to imitate the appearance of lace.

Layered: Describing a fashion look in which layers of clothing are worn in noticeably different lengths.

Leg warmer: Tube-shaped sock worn above the ankle to keep legs warm.

Leotard: A one-piece, close-fitting body suit, like a swimsuit; used by dancers.

Liberty print: Small flower patterns from the Liberty Company of England.

Lingerie: Women's decorative underwear, such as a camisole, emphasizing femininity.

Loafers: Slip-on shoes without laces.

Loose fit: Too-large clothing, worn intentionally; also associated with the Japanese bag-lady look popular in the early eighties.

Loungewear: Casual clothes usually worn around the home and not on the street. Popular loungewear pieces include caftans and long, loose-fitting dresses.

Lycee: A fashion look based on the casual clothing of secondary-school-age girls in Paris. The look is sweet and stylish and includes a beret, a low-waisted, pleated jumper, and a white blouse with a large collar.

Macramé: Course thread knotted to make decorative belts, bags, and other things.

Madras: A cotton cloth—first produced in Madras, India—of multicolored plaid patterns. Used to make shirts and skirts. The colors will sometimes bleed (run together) when the garment is washed.

Maillot: A woman's one-piece bathing suit having a classic and simple style that is without embellishment and emphasizes the natural shape of the body.

Masculine: Male; describing women's clothes that are tailored to resemble men's.

Marble print: A speckled pattern that imitates natural stone patterns; used in shoes, bags, and accessories.

Marine look: An appearance evoked by wearing a sailor suit or any clothing reminiscent of a nautical style; spring/summer fashion employing a sailor collar, anchor or boat motifs, and a blue and white color palette.

Merchandising: The presentation of new products. All aspects of a product, including design, quality, and consumer demand, must be considered.

Mesh net: A net usually found in summer bags or shoes; can be decorative or functional for ventilation.

Military look: An appearance designed to imitate an element of the military.

Milk tone: A soft off-white; meant to be added to other colors.

Mismatched: Unexpectedly matched. Combinations such as a silk blouse with a leather jacket, lace worn with mannish pants, plaids with tweeds, and two different weaves in the same ensemble.

Moccasins: Casual shoes of soft leather; first worn by native Americans.

Mode: Fashion; originally, haute couture.

Modernism: Fashion in the twenties and thirties that emphasized function.

Mod look: Fashion from London's Carnaby Street; marked by flower prints and color combinations; also, European-styled suits.

Monotone: A single color; a black or white color scheme.

Natural colors: Colors, soft in hue and image, relating to beige. These colors are popular choices for linen and summer fashion. Grey, soft blue, pink, peach, off-white, and beige are the important natural colors.

Natural fibers: Cotton, silk, wool, and linen, all of which occur in nature. The opposite of fibers which are made from synthetics or chemicals.

Neoclassic: Designating modern styles that incorporate traditional design ideas.

Neoromanticism: Modern design that incorporates elements of fantasy and imagination.

Neutral colors: Non-colors; colors without hue and visible wavelength. Black, white, and grey are true neutrals. Adding black or white to a pure color lightens or darkens it, neutralizing the pure hue.

New wave: The fashion trend, originating in London, that followed punk fashion; emphasis on extreme, brash fashion.

Nostalgia: A longing for the past. A revival fashion evoking images of the twenties, thirties, fifties, and sixties.

Oxford: Describing cloth that has a diagonal weave and is named for the town and university of Oxford, England. Originally, this cloth was used for the tennis wear of the university team.

Paisley: Printed with leaf patterns. Originally from ancient India and Persia, paisley designs were popularized by 18th-century wool weavers in Paisley, Scotland. The paisley pattern has both an ethnic and an exotic quality.

Panache: Originally, a small feather plume; now, dash or style.

Pastel color: A pale, soft color made by adding white to a bright color; a color typical of spring.

Pastoral print: A design showing a landscape scene; often used in T-shirt designs.

Patchwork: A folk design made from sewing small patches of cloth together; traditionally used for cushion and bed covers but now also used for accessories and embroidered clothes.

Peasant look: An appearance created from a romantic image of simplicity, usually with a full skirt and embroidered blouse.

Peter Pan collar: A round shirt collar; often used in children's clothing.

Plain: Simple; not decorative; neat.

Polo shirt: Originally, a shirt worn for polo playing; now, fashionable sportswear, often with a small logo on the chest pocket.

Poor (cheap) chic: Fashion created from cheap clothes, often from secondhand stores.

Post-modern: Describing a trend that emphasizes decoration, as opposed to modernism's emphasis on function.

Preppie: Son of Ivy League; a collegiate look characterized by polo shirts, chinos, and navy blazers. Ralph Lauren is the sitting god to the preppies.

Pret-a-porter: Ready to wear; can be popular styles or haute couture.

Primary colors: Red, blue, and yellow. All other colors are derived from these three colors.

Print-on-print: Having one pattern printed on a contrasting pattern—for example, flowers on stripes, wearing different patterns together.

Psychedelic: Relating to hallucinatory drugs popular in the sixties among hippies and artists. Effects on the fashion world included acidic colors, strange prints, and body painting.

Pullover: An outer layer, usually a sweater, without buttons.

Pure color: The clearest color value.

Raglan sleeve: A sleeve with slanted seams extending from the underarm to the neck; for comfortable jackets and coats.

Receding color: A dark color or color value that appears smaller than it really is because it seems to reduce or minimize.

Regimental stripe: A necktie design of stripes in the colors of British military flags; red, blue, or green stripes on a dark blue background.

Resort wear: Casual clothes—T-shirts, sundresses, swimwear, and shorts—for poolside or winter vacations in sunny climates.

Reversible: Wearable with either side out.

Rugger (rugby) shirt: A long-sleeved, horizontally striped shirt worn by rugby players.

Sack dress (chemise): Sixties-style, loose-fitting dress that was slipped on over the head.

Saddle shoes: Saddle oxford shoes; two-color shoes—white with black or with brown.

Safari look: A style derived from clothing worn for hunting big game in Africa; a jacket with patch pockets and a belt, usually in khaki-colored cloth.

Sailor collar: A collar that is V-shaped in front and square in back; part of the marine look.

Scottish: Pertaining to Scotland; Scottish folk styles include tartan kilts, vests, knee socks, and Fair Isle sweaters.

Secondary colors: Orange, green, and violet. Colors made by combining two primary colors: yellow and red make orange; blue and yellow make green; red and blue make violet.

Seamless: Without seams; for example, seamless stockings, bras, knit skirts and sweaters.

Seasonless dressing: A dressing style made up of clothes that work regardless of the time of year; for example, a rayon dress.

Seersucker: Literally, "milk and sugar." Crinkled material, usually made of linen or cotton; ideal for summer.

Semiformal: Describing a dress code requiring a single-or double-breasted black suit for men, an evening or cocktail dress for women.

Shaggy: Long-haired; for example, angora or mohair.

Shetland: Wool or woolen textiles produced in Scotland; ideal material for a sweater or a coat.

Silhouette: Outline; the lay of the material; the shape of a garment.

Slim: Slender; sleek linear style.

Slip-on: Describing clothing put on over the head or shoes without laces or buckles, that is, loafers.

Slub: To allow the natural character of a fiber to show up in the surface of a weave.

Solid color: A single color without print or pattern.

Sophisticated: Urban and stylish.

Spencer: A long-sleeved, short jacket, first worn by the Earl of Spencer in 19th century England.

Stadium (letterman) jacket: A sporty jacket, usually made of satin or flannel, with sleeves of a contrasting color. Originally, a baseball player's training jacket, often labeled with the school or team name.

Stone wash: Repeated washing of a fabric to fade the color; the effect of putting a stone in the washing machine with the clothes.

Strapless: Without straps; usually describing a dress for evening wear.

Stylist: A specialist who coordinates clothes and creates styles or looks; different from a designer.

Success dressing: Fashion with a yuppie influence for business or professional women; derived from men's fashion but softened with pleated skirts and feminine blouses.

Summer darks: Dark colors and black used for summer wear; usually made of cotton or linen.

Surfer look: Originally, a fashion worn by young people who surfed; now a popular active sport and resort look.

Sweats: Cotton jersey sportswear.

Synthetic fiber: Fiber with no natural origin, such as rayon, acetate, nylon, vinyl, and acrylic.

Tailored: Fashioned or fitted; usually refers to men's styles. Tailored styles follow a set design and have enduring wearability.

Textiles: General term for raw material and woven cloth.

Texture: Woven cloth or the character of the cloth.

Thirties fashion: A style featuring long, slim lines and feminine bias cuts.

Tiered look: A fashion for skirts and dresses composed of bands of gathered cloth.

Tone-on-tone: Slight variation in the shade of a single color. Pattern or effect created by using a lighter shade of color on a darker value of the same color.

Top: An item of clothing worn above the waist; for example a blouse or a jacket.

Total look: The appearance evoked by wearing a unified, coordinated outfit.

Town wear: Street clothes.

Transparency: A texture so fine that it can be seen through. Gauzes and Georgettes are popular examples of transparent materials.

Transsexual fashion: A style that is neither male or female; beyond distinguishing male from female fashion; same as unisex.

Trendies: Fashion groupies who slavishly follow every new fashion movement.

Tricolor: The red, white, and blue colors of the French flag.

T-shape: A design that stretches across the shoulders and tapers downward.

Tweed: Rough wool cloth originally woven in Scotland; for jackets, pants, and skirts.

Twin prints: Two prints, such as a stripe and a dot, that share the same color combination. Twin prints are often used in the same garment.

Vogue: Fashionable. The fashion magazine *Vogue* reports designer fashion trends to sophisticated consumers in French, British, American, Italian, Australian, and Japanese editions.

Wardrobe: A planned assortment of clothes; a dresser or cabinet to store clothes in.

Warm colors: Colors with a red or yellow undertone and suggesting an energetic and upbeat image. The basic warm colors are red, orange, and yellow.

Waterproof: Impervious to water; can refer to clothing or cosmetics.

Wraparound skirt: One piece of material that wraps around the lower half of the body and fastens at the waist.

Wrap coat: A coat without buttons or fasteners; can be tied with a sash or worn open.

Yuppie: A Young Urban Professional; describing clothes worn by yuppies, whose annual income is said to be equal their age times $2,000. Legend has it that yuppies wear Ralph Lauren, Burberry, and Rolex watches; and they carry Gucci briefcases.